Teaching to Justice, Citizenship, and Civic Virtue

Teaching to Justice, Citizenship, and Civic Virtue
The Character of a High School Through the Eyes of Faith

By Julia K. Stronks
and Gloria Goris Stronks

RESOURCE *Publications* · Eugene, Oregon

TEACHING TO JUSTICE, CITIZENSHIP, AND CIVIC VIRTUE
The Character of a High School Through the Eyes of Faith

Copyright © 2014 Wipf and Stock Publishers. All rights reserved. Except for brief quotations in critical publications or reviews, no part of this book may be reproduced in any manner without prior written permission from the publisher. Write: Permissions. Wipf and Stock Publishers, 199 W. 8th Ave., Suite 3, Eugene, OR 97401.

Wipf and Stock
An Imprint of Wipf and Stock Publishers
199 W. 8th Ave., Suite 3
Eugene, OR 97401

www.wipfandstock.com

ISBN 13: 978-1-62564-785-6

Manufactured in the U.S.A.   09/15/2014

THE HOLY BIBLE, NEW INTERNATIONAL VERSION®, NIV® Copyright © 1973, 1978, 1984, 2011 by Biblica, Inc.® Used by permission. All rights reserved worldwide.

We attended Christian schools, taught at Christian schools, and sent our children to Christian schools. This book is dedicated to all the wonderful teachers in our lives.

Micah 6:8

He has shown you, O mortal, what is good.
And what does the Lord require of you?
To act justly and to love mercy
And to walk humbly with your God.

Contents

Introduction: Midland Christian High School | ix

1. The Outcomes of a Christian Education | 1
2. The Mission of a Christian School | 6
3. The Teenage Brain as a Work in Progress | 15
4. Before Empathy | 24
5. Anatomy of a Judgment | 34
6. A Theology of Citizenship | 43
7. Engaging Culture—History, Politics, and Technology | 50
8. Engaging Culture—Dealing with Difference | 68
9. Engaging Culture—The Arts and Business | 78
10. Athletics in a Christian High School | 91
11. Life after High School | 103
12. Life-long Learning | 115

Conclusion: Learning from Others—Revelation and Response | 128
Bibliography | 133

Introduction
Midland Christian High School

IN THE TWO DECADES since the publication of *A Vision With A Task: Christian Schooling for Responsive Discipleship* (Stronks and Blomberg 1993), there have been many changes in the lives and culture of Christian high school students. According to the Beloit Mindset list, this year's seniors are more interested in having their own cell phone and Skype accounts than in getting a driver's license and car. Students have always been able to read books electronically; the U.S. has always been at war, and females have always outnumbered males in college. In addition, students are well-connected with each other through the use of smartphones and texting, but they do not always use technology wisely.

Teachers are faced with the best ways to use the varieties of technology available to enhance student learning. They are aware that much of the contact students have with each other happens not face-to-face but while staring at a screen. Parents continue to wonder about the role of athletics in the lives of students, and in a changing economy, administrators and school boards are faced with new problems.

At the time of the publication of *Vision*, we said that in the Christian school the roles of "conserver, discerner, and reformer" come together in a full-orbed life of responsive discipleship. Both individually and communally, we unwrap God's gifts, share each other's burdens, and work for *shalom*. We were talking about the entire culture of the school.

So, what does it take to develop the culture of a school? Midland Christian High School, the setting of this book, is fictional; however, it is drawn from our own experiences as we have worked with teachers and schools through the years. Midland is designed to show how a group of teachers and administrators might plan together to meet the challenges

Introduction

of the day while working toward God's *shalom* in a broken but redeemed world. We want to present ways faculty can implement some of the changes they believe are in keeping with the goals of their school.

Here the teachers and administrators at Midland consider the mission and outcomes of Christian education. They look at today's student asking questions about how students learn and what students need to figure out what God is requiring of them. The teachers hear from experts in the fields of civic education, art, politics, business, technology, and athletics. Finally, they talk about their own learning and what they want students to know about life after high school.

We hope this book will be of help to Christian teachers in different kinds of schools and also that it will serve parents who are home schooling their children.

Midland Christian High School Cast of Characters:

Tom Anderson, principal
Bonnie Hendricks, guidance counselor
Sue Jamison, Brian Chase, Andrea James, fifteen-year teaching veterans
Joe Sand, twenty-year teaching veteran
Joy Storey, new teacher and former attorney
David Barnes, new teacher and former business owner
and military veteran

1

Outcomes of Christian Education

THE MORNING DEVOTIONS HAD *come to an end at the first Midland Christian High School faculty meeting of the year, and the teachers were engaged in an introductory "meet and greet" time over coffee.*

"Well, here we go again for what it's worth," muttered Joe as he set his coffee down on the table beside Sue.

"That doesn't sound very encouraging," laughed Sue.

"I just can't help it," Joe said softly. "I looked in the mirror this morning and wondered whether I actually have it in me to do this for one more year." He saw Sue's startled expression. "Sorry, but I keep wondering whether this is all worthwhile. So much money goes into keeping this school going. Is it really that important that these kids attend a Christian high school? Many of them come from Christian homes. The elementary school has given them a good foundation. Maybe the time has come for them all to go to a state school, and we could send the money it takes to run this place to some mission program."

"We have to talk more about this," said Sue. "Also, I've been hearing rumors about some changes. There was talk about some of us getting pink slipped, but that must not have happened since all of us are here except for those who retired or took the early retirement deal the board offered. But right now it looks as though Anderson is giving the signal for us to go back to work."

Principal Tom Anderson began the next session by saying, "Some tough decisions were made during the summer months because of the lagging economy, and one of them was that some of the retirees would not be replaced. I'm grateful to those of you who have agreed to teach subjects you haven't taught before just to make things work. We've been careful to keep state certification in mind so that the classes could be covered by people who are certified to teach them.

Teaching to Justice, Citizenship, and Civic Virtue

"I'm also grateful to the Faculty Committee who worked with the board to make some interesting decisions for change. On their recommendation, we've hired two new people who will, we hope, provide a different kind of leadership. The first of these is David Barnes. Some of you may remember that Dave graduated from Midland twelve years ago. Since that time he has spent four years in the military, eight years in business, and then earned a Master of Arts in Teaching from one of our Christian colleges. David will be teaching in the sciences and helping out in math as needed."

"Just what we need, a drill sergeant," muttered Joe.

"Our other new hire," continued Anderson, "is Joy Storey. Joy is an attorney and spent eight years in practice with a large corporate law firm out east. She and David were both participants in the same MAT program, and she will be teaching in the humanities."

"You will get to know Joy and David as time goes by. However, right now we must get on with the program for today. Bonnie Hendricks, our guidance counselor, has gathered some research that will jumpstart an ongoing conversation about what we are doing here at Midland High. Bonnie, you need no introduction to this group, so why don't you begin?"

Bonnie gathered her notes and walked to the front of the room.

"Thank you, Tom. I came across some interesting research this summer, and I think the results might have implications for some discussions we have been having. You may have heard of the Cardus Education Survey. The researchers addressed the question, 'Do the motivations for private religious Catholic and Protestant Schooling in North America align with graduate outcomes?' We have ordered several copies of the results of this survey so that you can read about it for yourself. In looking at this research, we will want to discuss what the actual purpose of Christian education is."

In the *Cardus Education Survey,* researchers surveyed adults between the ages of twenty-three and forty-nine who had graduated from Catholic and Protestant schools, home-schools, and state schools. They measured three outcomes of Christian education: spiritual formation, cultural engagement, and academic development. These are their general findings:

1. The authors found that there were significant differences in outcomes between Catholic and Protestant schools. Catholic schools emphasized academic outcomes more strongly which resulted in graduates that earned higher household incomes and more graduate degrees. Catholic school graduates are more likely to engage in political

protests and make political contributions than other students; however, this comes at the expense of developing faith, commitment to religious practices, and accepting the authority of church leadership.

2. Protestant Christian school graduates are more likely to have a vibrant religious and spiritual life, attend religious services, and want a job that is helpful to others rather than one that primarily pays well. They are likely to have a large family, believe the Bible is infallible, give financial donations to charity, believe that living together before marriage is wrong, and believe that divorce is morally wrong. They tend to be prepared for relationships. However, they are less likely to make political contributions and engage in boycotts or political protests. They are also less likely to attend more prestigious colleges and universities.

3. These days we have increasing numbers of students who are homeschooled. The survey showed that these graduates are more likely to want a job that pays well, have a vibrant religious and spiritual life, attend church, believe the Bible is infallible, and marry young. These graduates are less likely to feel prepared for college, less likely to spend time volunteering, more likely to feel helpless in dealing with the problems of life. The survey suggested that often they appear to lack clear goals or sense of direction.

4. Christian graduates who attended public schools were also considered. The survey showed they are more likely to appreciate new and exciting experiences, actively campaign for a political party and be interested in political matters, and feel prepared for college; however, they are less likely to feel prepared for relationships and less likely to have a vibrant religious and spiritual life.

In another interesting study, Kevin Den Dulk and Jonathan Hill, Calvin College professors, asked whether the kind of school a student goes to impacts the level of voluntarism among graduates. They looked at a huge survey called the National Study of Youth and Religion and analyzed the data from a variety of different perspectives. First, they found that just under half of the adults in the study continued volunteering after high school. They also found that after controlling for family backgrounds, economics, and other variables, the kind of school that a student attended actually had a big impact on adult behavior. The results were so strong that the authors were surprised. Young adults who had gone to protestant Christian schools were almost three times more likely to be involved in volunteering than those who had gone to public schools. Those who had gone to Catholic schools were more likely to be involved in volunteering than those at public schools, and those who had been home-schooled were half as likely as public school kids to volunteer. Those who had gone to non-religious private schools were the least likely to be involved in volunteering.

The outcomes of these surveys generalize graduates, but surveys like this help us to think through the connection between what we *think* we are doing and what impact our schools actually have on our alumni. It seems important that we ask ourselves what tendencies we hope to see in people who graduate from our schools and are now between the ages of twenty-three and forty-nine.

- What are they doing, and what aspects of our school affected their lives?
- What about the culture of our school was important to them?
- Do we care about having our graduates involved in volunteering? Do we want them to be involved in politics? In the mission field? In working toward justice and *shalom*?
- If so, how do we measure this desire?
- How do we work toward these goals?

Tom Anderson walked to the front of the room.

"Thank you, Bonnie. What we don't know is to what extent the findings of the Cardus Education Survey reflect what is happening in our own school. So, let's talk about it. I'd like to center our discussion on our own goals and what we do here at Midland Christian High."

After a lengthy discussion Tom said, "After listening to you, it seems to me that we are all hoping to change and improve the culture here in our school. I would like it if during the next two weeks you would, in light of our discussion today, provide our Faculty Committee with questions or topics you would like to have addressed at future meetings."

When teachers, parents and administrators consider the *Cardus Education Survey* they have to think about the implications of these findings for their own schools. The Midland faculty will be considering the following topics:
- Which of the trends seen in the *Cardus Education Survey* are in accordance with the goals for our school? Are there additional trends we should consider?

Outcomes of Christian Education

- Are we stressing intellectual development and academic performance as much as we should? Have our expectations for superior academic performance been too limited? What indications do we have that will help us know to what extent that is or isn't true?
- Do our students have questions that are not presently addressed anywhere in our curriculum? How can we discover what those questions might be?
- Do our graduates leave with an understanding of how to address the big questions that are part of living as Christians in a democracy? Do they understand that moral values include knowing how to address big questions that concern justice and responsibility?
- How do the arts, technology, and business impact the world in which our students live? Do they have the skills they need to engage the culture in these fields?
- While parents and the community love attending competitive sports events, do competitive team sports have any real value in the intellectual, emotional, moral, or spiritual lives of our students?
- Do our graduates leave with some idea of their future career path and the kind of preparation that will need? Can we do a better job of helping them plan their future?

The *Cardus Education Survey* can be accessed at http://www.cardus.ca/research/education/publications/surveys/

2

The Mission of a Christian School

Several years ago, we were sitting with a group of parents watching some of the 1,500 three-person teams playing at Hoopfest, Spokane's annual event encouraging people of all ages and abilities to play basketball. All the parents were Christians. Some were home-schooling, some had their children in the public school, and others had children in a Christian high school. The discussion got a little heated.

"The reason we home-school our children is because we want to be the only ones to influence their thinking. Christian schools aren't really any different than public schools. There are drugs and sex and all sorts of problems."

"I'm not sure that in our society it is even possible for parents to be the only ones to influence their children's thinking. That's the reason we want our children to be at the local Christian high school, even though the financial cost is enormous and requires sacrifice on our part. Of course there are problems, but our hope is that our children will understand biblical ways of thinking about all aspects of life."

"Well, aside from the cost of your choices, both personal and financial, I would be uneasy isolating my children from the community the way you are. If we want our children to live as Christians in a secular world, it seems to me they should begin while they are still in school. Our kids go to the public school and have a chance to share their faith. Besides, I can't really see how young people who leave your Christian school differ from other young Christians. You can see problems among the kids in both groups."

There are few things more important to Christian parents than their children's education and well-being; however, parental discussion of the most suitable institutions of education for children is often more anecdotal than factual. Findings of the *Cardus Education Survey* have not only opened up a much-needed discussion but also provided important information for parents as well as for teachers.

Over the course of the last few decades, many schools have focused on character education. Schools have worked to foster moral or civic virtues in teenagers, and service-learning or volunteer programs have become mandatory in many high schools. Recently, there has been more emphasis on an intellectual virtues education model. Schools are looking at intellectual virtues like curiosity, intellectual humility and rigor, intellectual thoroughness, and care. But what does this mean for Christian high schools? Are we to do the same or are there other things Christians should focus on? What is the mission of a Christian high school?

Andrea: Tom Anderson told me that the Midland school board questioned him concerning whether the students in our classes are being taught to witness for their faith. Board members also had a disagreement about whether teaching students to witness is the role of the school or the church. Tom suggested to them that the matter be brought to the faculty since we are the professionals concerning teaching and learning. That is the background for the discussion we are having in this meeting.

Joy: I knew the matter would be before us, so I checked the mission statement. It didn't really provide much clarity. If we are, as we say, helping our students learn to impact culture, discussions of the life of faith certainly are important. I assume this involves developing the ability to talk to others about our faith.

Brian: In my social studies class, we have been talking about what it means to love the Lord our God with all our heart, soul, strength, and mind and to love our neighbor as ourselves. But one pretty brave student said it is really difficult to have the "feelings" of faith. Lots of students agreed with him.

David: This is tough. In many ways, actions lead to feelings. Perhaps we might begin with the premise that the life of faith includes words and actions. The life of faith is more than words, but it must include words. It is more than actions, but it must include actions. That is why virtue education is so important in a Christian school.

Sue: Must the actions of faith always be accompanied by the words of faith? If I am helpful to someone in need, must I always tell that person it is because I believe that is how Jesus wants me to act?

Joe: That sounds pietistic. So much of that kind of talk can turn people away.

Teaching to Justice, Citizenship, and Civic Virtue

>   *Brian:* I've been thinking that the role of the school is to help students learn the actions that are part of the faith life. I agree with David that feelings often result from actions. I mean, feelings result from actions that take place in the hallways, on the playing field, in the classroom, in service activities, and elsewhere.
>
>   *Joe:* And we are saying that while both the words and the actions are part of the life of faith, they don't always have to occur at the same time.
>
>   *Joy:* Loving my neighbor, then, is not geographical. It is making God's presence known to others in different ways and at different times. As a teacher, I can try with all my might to arrange my instructional activities so my students will learn to live with the words and actions of the life of faith. I can make assignments with that as my goal. I can do my best to insist on good and kind behavior on the part of the students, but I have no control over whether students internalize the importance of witnessing to others using the words and actions of the life of faith. I have no control over whether or not they have the "feelings" of faith.
>
>   *Andrea:* That sounds like a good response to the questions the board members asked, but I do not think it is going to solve the disagreement. Many people think evangelizing is the purpose of all that we do on this earth.

It's hard to know how to solve a debate like that of the school board members. Parents and teachers around the world will always have different opinions about the mission of a Christian school, but we can learn a great deal from those who have studied Scripture and education over the decades. In this area, one name stands out as particularly helpful.

Nicholas Wolterstorff, the Noah Porter Emeritus Professor of Philosophical Theology at Yale, has written for years on the purpose of education through the eyes of faith. He says that all Christians are struggling to ask fundamental questions: Who are we? What are we here for? How should we connect to what seems like a very secular society?

His answer is interesting: We must seek God's *shalom*.

In Scripture, we see God's vision for human flourishing. *Shalom* invokes an image of people living in right relationships with God, themselves, each other, and nature. We are taking delight in and celebrating all that God has created. Sadly, we live in a society that is filled with pain, suffering, and brokenness; but if we believe in the redemption of Jesus Christ, we are free to seek *reconciliation* in this world while we wait for Christ's return.

Wolterstorff argues that the task of Christian education is to prepare students to be able to seek God's justice, reconciliation, and *shalom* in all parts of life. He has said so often words to this effect, "What I mean is that we must not just teach *about* justice – though we must; I mean we must teach *for* justice. The graduate whom we seek to produce must be one who *practices* justice."

Grounding his plea in Biblical guidance, Wolterstorff provides six theological principles as foundation for his argument.[1]

1. *A good creation:* What God produced was good. God is working through us using Christ's redemption and common grace to sustain the world.

2. *The holistic effects of evil and sin:* Sin impacts everything. It hurts our will, our reason, our technology, our conversations, our relationships, our social structures. Every part of life is broken.

3. *The holistic scope of Christ's redemption:* God as the Creator of all things is also the Redeemer and Reconciler of all things fallen. Even though all parts of creation have been impacted by the fall, they are also impacted by Christ's redemption. We have hope.

4. *Authentic faith is not an addendum to our lives but is holistic and pervasive:* Faith is not just the saving of lost souls, but it is renewal and redemption of all of creation.

5. *God's Sovereignty over all of life:* As we teach we must help students understand what this means for every part of the world they come into contact with.

6. *God's Lordship is over all the earth:* Our work and the work that students do now and in the future must be responsive to God. Responding to God often means standing against some of the forces of a broken culture.

The key for Wolterstorff is to start with an important question: What is our image of a successful graduate? He wants us to cultivate in students the disposition to work and pray for *shalom*. He encourages us to help students recognize when *shalom* is missing, to grieve when it is absent, and to celebrate *shalom's* presence.

Christian education has to be centered on seeking the Kingdom of God. We prepare students for life and work in God's Kingdom, and students

---

1. Joldersma and Stronks, *Educating for Shalom*.

have to be equipped to be responsible agents in this world. Teachers, then, have the honor and responsibility to develop in students dispositions necessary to be citizens that seek justice on behalf of others. To do this, they must be able to recognize injustice and have the skills to think through what a just society might look like. We do this through our talents in business and the arts, as citizens, psychologists, waiters, and scientists.

Wolterstorff asks us to keep these four themes in mind for all areas that we teach:[2]

- Reasons: Students need reasons to act a particular way, and the reasons have to be connected to their worldviews or deep religious convictions.
- Discipline: Students must find joy for themselves in learning and truthtelling. They must also learn to feel sorrow and be energized to make change when they see evidence that *shalom* has been broken.
- Modeling: Students will learn to act justly and to struggle toward justice if they see us and our institutions doing the same. We must teach to justice, live for justice, and struggle toward justice.
- Empathy: Students have to learn to put themselves in the place of others. One of the best ways to do this is to present the human faces of those who suffer to our students.

How Do We Start?

Working toward justice and engaging culture is complex partly because it is hard to do and partly because it can be scary. Though parents, administrators, and teachers might have the desire that their students impact culture, the *Cardus Education Survey* demonstrated that this rarely happens. Few schools were found to be systematically, through curriculum and pedagogy, integrating academic learning with engaging the world outside of school. Instead, schools seem to rely on teachers to "spontaneously make connections" when an opportunity arises. Interactions with the world are only rarely integrated into the curriculum; rather, the focus is on volunteering in the community or field trips.

If we are going to challenge ourselves on the seeking of *shalom* there are some steps that we can take. The first thing to do is to be sure teachers and parents are on the same page. This means that everyone must be able

---

2. Joldersma and Stronks, *Educating for Shalom*.

to articulate the mission of the school and should be able to talk about what worldview is. That will not be as easy as it sounds because a biblical worldview is likely to be in conflict with the worldviews of some parents who believe that the real importance of education is to prepare students to find positions and contacts that will ensure they make a great deal of money. At the same time, other parents may have the concerns the school board of Midland High School outlined at the beginning of this chapter. The conflict between thinking of a school as a place to train evangelizers and a place to help students think about seeking God's *shalom* has to be put right on the table and discussed by everyone.

We think that the key is "putting it right on the table." We advise that teachers, parents, administrators, school board members, and students all engage in an annual discussion about what worldview is and how it is relevant to the work students are doing.

Here is one way to approach the worldview challenge: invite the community into a worldview forum. Structure it by talking about worldview. Have community members work to articulate their own worldviews, and have demonstrations about how worldview has shaped students' world.

Beginning the Conversation: What is a Worldview?

Everyone, religious or not, has a worldview—a foundational set of beliefs by which we seek to make sense of the world around us. Often we are not cognizant of our worldview; nonetheless, our beliefs and experiences help us to answer some of the most important questions in life:

- What does it mean to be human?
- Are people basically good or bad?
- What went wrong in the world?
- Can what went wrong ever be made right?
- What is my job in this world? How shall I live?

There is a very real connection between worldviews and ways of life. They always inform each other. What we believe is most clearly seen in how we live, and continuing to live in a particular way deepens and strengthens our worldview. When someone's actions and conversations reflect a strong desire to connect what they believe about the world with how they live in the world, we recognize that they have woven about them something that Steve Garber has called a "fabric of faithfulness."

To move in this direction, we need to ask ourselves questions such as: Are my beliefs best seen from actions that I refrain from doing, or are they best revealed in actions that I do? We should ask and answer those questions, because the decisions we make for ourselves will either nourish or destroy our connection with others.

If teachers want to encourage students to engage the world, they have to think about it in phases. First, students have to be aware of culture. They critique it, and finally they can be involved in thinking about how to challenge and change it.

If teachers are to guide students in this process, it presupposes that the teachers themselves have an understanding of what it means to think as a Christian about the biggest problems of the world through the eyes of faith. With all that teachers do with our students it is too much to expect them to have this all figured out. Fortunately, there are many different experts available to help teachers talk with students about Christian approaches to cultural challenges. Organizations like *Center for Public Justice*, *Sojourners*, *Evangelicals for Social Action*, social media groups like *ThinkChristian.org* and magazines like *Relevant* are filled with Christian perspectives on social problems. Teachers can use these and also ask authors to "visit" their classrooms through Skype so students can talk with people who devote their lives to engaging and changing culture in a broken but redeemed world.

Ideally, with the support of the administration, the teachers could get together and blend classes to do this. We have found that it is very difficult to get an entire school on board. This does not mean, however, that a small group of teachers can't band together to link their classes and still make a profound difference in the analytical ability of their students. We have found that when students are exposed to this kind of work, they like it so much that their enthusiasm can start a chain reaction influencing the curriculum of other teachers.

The rest of this book is organized to help the community conversation about worldview and engaging culture. First, we have to think about how teenagers learn and what they think they want to learn about. Then we can start to look at different content areas through the eyes of faith.

Tom Anderson: I appreciate the thinking you are all doing about the mission of our school. During his graduate program in teaching, one of our new teachers worked with a group of colleagues on the concept of blended classes to improve integrative thinking. Dave, will you tell us a little about it?

Dave: *Well, keep in mind that I'm a new kid on the block here, so I want to learn from all of you, but I hope I have a few things to add as well. I had a career in business before I became a teacher, and one of the things that was hard for us as employers was that kids that came to us didn't know how to look at a problem from a variety of perspectives. Some of that is a lack of empathy, as we have been discussing. Some of it was also a lack of integrative thinking. So the people I worked with in graduate school were trying to come up with ways to involve a whole school in tackling a problem. And, how great it would be to do it through the eyes of faith!*

Take an issue like sex-trafficking, for example. Over the course of a semester, teachers in all fields could commit to exploring the issue of trafficking from the perspective of their own subjects: history of trafficking in the country, the economics of trafficking, the psychological impact of this sort of violence on victims, literature about violence can be explored, the sociological or legal aspects of trafficking, and biblical principles that relate to violence against the weak. Since trafficking exists in every country and most cities, experts can be brought in to talk with students in person or via Skype. Students can explore what sorts of groups exist in their own community to treat victims or prosecute criminals in this field. Finally, students can research and discuss how the everyday activities we engage in might have the unanticipated consequences of supporting the traffickers themselves. For example, sometimes pedicure/manicure salons or certain kinds of restaurants secretly engage in trafficked labor. I don't know what you are all thinking about this. It wouldn't have to involve everyone if there wasn't a lot of excitement over it, but, if anyone is interested in blending classes in this way I'd love to work on it with you.

Discussion Questions

1. What is the mission of your school? Do you think parents can articulate it?
2. Where is your school community on the issue of whether a school should teach students to evangelize, be prepared to make money, or be prepared to seek *shalom* in the world?

Teaching to Justice, Citizenship, and Civic Virtue

3. Are there ways in which your school is already helping students to think about justice, or ways in which your school helps students to delight in God's creation?
4. What does *worldview* mean in your community? Have you ever hosted a discussion for parents about this?

Examining My Worldview

- What things do I truly believe are worth caring about?
- Which things in my life matter the most to me?
- What do I believe is wrong with the world?
- What could I do to repair what is wrong? What could others do?
- What do I think is the job of the church? What about business? Art?
- Is it true that what I believe can be seen in how I live?
- What are ways in which my beliefs are revealed in actions that I
- refrain from doing?
- What are ways in which my beliefs are revealed in actions that I do?

3

The Teenage Brain as a Work in Progress

"If a teen is doing music, sports, or academics, those are the connections that will be hard wired. If they are lying on the couch or playing video games or watching MTV, those are the cells and connections that are going to survive."

—JAY GIEDD

AFTER THE BRIEF BUSINESS *part of the meeting was completed, Tom Anderson asked Andrea to report on the continuing work of the faculty committee.*

While she distributed parts of her report to the faculty, Andrea said, "You will remember that during the first two weeks of this academic year, we were each asked to submit questions or topics we would like to have addressed at future faculty meetings. One of the most frequently submitted topics concerned whether our students have questions that are not presently addressed anywhere in our curriculum and how we might discover what those questions are.

"With the help of the student council members we looked for ways to determine the kinds of questions our students might ask. We began by reading through Essenburg's 99 Biblical Perspective Questions that we found on his blog. The students thought that while many of the questions were important to them, there were also likely other questions that they and other students in our school have.

The student council came up with the following questions they would like to have addressed in their classes:

- How should we deal with injustice?
- Why is it important to be aware of the culture of others?

Teaching to Justice, Citizenship, and Civic Virtue

- *How can art express a person's beliefs?*
- *What does it mean to have a biblical perspective?*
- *How can learning a second language change you?*
- *What does it mean to love your neighbor as yourself?*
- *How does God use ordinary people to work in the world?*
- *Can I be a Christian if I want to win and beat the other guy?*
- *Why are Christians so angry in politics? Which side is right?*
- *What should I consider when thinking about a career?*
- *I don't want to go to college yet, but I don't feel prepared for the working world. What should I do?*

Tom said, "Are you suggesting that we divide these questions up and address them in specific classes?"

"Not at all," Andrea replied. "In fact, the faculty committee and student council members said that is exactly what we should not do. Instead we might find ways to address some of these questions as they seem appropriate in our regular classes."

"Wow," Joe exclaimed, "Some of these are questions I've had during most of my life. How in the world can I help students with answers?" Others nodded their agreement.

The students' questions highlight a couple of important things. First, high school students are concerned about their own faith. Second, students themselves are concerned about culture.

Michael Essenburg says in his blog that *commitment results in action*.[3] So when we want to know how committed we are to something, we have to look at what we are doing. At Christian schools, we're committed to helping students connect what they study with what the Bible teaches. Essenburg says that, in his experience, teachers who are committed to using questions to help students make connections take action:

- They have identified effective Biblical perspective questions like, "How can you relate to culture?"
- They frame each of their classes and each of their units around their Biblical perspective questions.

3. Essenburg, *Empowering Christian Leaders and Organizations to Close the Rhetoric/reality Gap Now.*

- They have students journal on a question.
- They use questions as a "springboard" to having their students read the Bible and articles by Christians.
- They use Biblical perspective questions as the basis of unit and semester assessments.
- They post their questions on a bulletin board and prominently feature their questions on their course syllabi and Web site.[4]

The questions the Midland students are asking are profoundly theological. Both they and we have to understand that answers evolve over time in different ways and at different levels of our faith development. Students and teachers must trust each other to confront hard questions. Parents and board members have to trust the teachers in this endeavor. Trust evolves from relationships, so it is critical that everyone in the process is attentive to building relationships between and among all the different participants in Christian schooling.

Moreover, high school students today are much more likely than their teachers or parents to one day work with people of a variety of races, to have female supervisors, and to work in communities where gay and transsexual citizens are open about their lives. They will face a world with little privacy, a lot of cheating, little trust, and changing social structures. Our students must be prepared to work across differences and must be able to think about what it means to do justice for people that have life experiences so different from their own.

The Brain of a Teenager

Andrea: I know things are changing for the students that we work with, but some things just never change. There are days when I can hardly get through to students, and yesterday was the pits. There are days when their curiosity amazes me, and there are days when their sullen faces make me want to smack them!

For more than twenty years, we have been aware of the changing and developing brain of the early adolescent. Teachers in Christian middle schools in Australia, Canada, and the United States have done some amazing work in

---

4. http://closethegapnow.org/blog/usequestions/files/7a9067c73b2c6824f6cfc066688daa34-56.html

creating classroom environments and instruction in ways that enhance the learner at that age instead of using the traditional "we must get them ready for high school" attitude of years past.

Only recently have we begun to understand that the moody, impulsive, reckless, and sometimes maddening actions of high school students may also be the key to success in their later adult years. It turns out that our brains take much longer to develop than we had thought.

The first full series of scans of the developing adolescent brain—a National Institutes of Health (NIH) project that studied over a hundred young people as they grew up during the 1990s—showed that our brains undergo a massive reorganization between our 12th and 25th years. The brain doesn't actually grow very much during this period. It has already reached 90 percent of its full size by the time a person is six, and a thickening skull accounts for most head growth afterward. As we move through adolescence, though, the brain undergoes extensive remodeling and resembles a network and wiring upgrade.

When this development proceeds normally, we get better at balancing impulse, desire, goals, self-interest, rules, ethics, and even altruism which generates behavior that is more complex and sometimes more sensible. At times, and especially at first, the brain does this work clumsily. It's hard to get all those new cogs to mesh.[5]

What complicates matters, however, is that these new abilities develop and mesh differently in different adolescents. The experiences and environments they encounter make a great deal of difference in their development. Along with this, the onset of puberty creates a tumult in which the young person's mental capacities do not move forward in a straight line.

Looking out at the faces in a typical high school class, a teacher will see bored and weary expressions but those expressions do not characterize adolescence. We look at those expressions and interpret them to be related to problems; however, the more we learn about this period, the more we are able to see that adolescence is really an important functional period for brain development. Their brains aren't finished developing yet but are perfectly suited for the job of separating from the home and moving into a wider world. The adolescent traits of looking for excitement, novelty, and risk are not simply cultural constructs. Culture influences adolescence, but these same traits appear in all countries and in all cultures. We already know that language learning is easier during the first thirteen years but

---

5. Dobbs, "Beautiful Brains," 48.

after that it becomes more difficult. In the same way, the brain in the late teens and early twenties heightens flexibility and that is necessary for learning. Arnett says that adults:

- Reach peak physical status between ages eighteen and thirty
- Reach peak visual acuity by about age twenty
- Reach peak auditory acuity before age twenty[6]

Learning During the Teenage Years

This is the first generation of teenagers that have any possible access to information about their own brain development. An important matter that can now be part of high school years is helping students understand their own minds and how they work. Researchers in adolescent brain development have helped us understand the following:

- There is exuberant growth during the pre-puberty years when the brain produces many more cells than it can use. There is not enough room in the skull for all of these cells and connections, so they compete with each other in order to survive. It is not true that by the time a child is seven years old the brain has fully formed. Recess, play, and everything that happens to that child really matters.
- During the high school years, there is a "pruning down" in which the cells and connections that are used will grow and strengthen while the cells and connections that are not used will be pruned away. Some people call this "brain sculpting." That's why a variety of high school activities such as athletics, academics, music, chess, and thinking exercises matter so much. This is also why we are concerned when there is too much watching TV, playing video games, and lying on the couch because those are the cells that are being strengthened with such activities.
- As a result of this pruning, some studies show that fourteen-year-olds recognize other people's emotions less than they did at the age of nine. It will take a few years before their growth and maturity allow them to do as well as their former selves in these areas.

---

6. Arnett, *Emerging Adulthood: The Winding Road from the Late Teens through the Twenties*.

- Doing drugs and alcohol during the teen years affect the adolescent brain for a longer period of time than for adults. What a teenager does on the weekend can truly affect how he or she does on a test the following Thursday.
- The prefrontal cortex, which governs reason and self-control, is the last region of the brain to become fully developed. Teenagers often rely on emotional reasons when making decisions, because the prefrontal regions of the brain, while functioning, are not yet fully developed.

Much of the factual knowledge students learn in school is forgotten within weeks. In addition to imparting facts, a teacher must work to shape the way students look at the world and to help them absorb the rules of history, or science, or any discipline.

When you praise students for their hard work, it reinforces their perception of themselves as industrious people. High self-esteem by itself should not be a goal but rather it should be the result of doing work well. Students become more motivated for doing good work when they are treated with respect and dignity.

High school students need to have a plan for the future because such plans help them transition through adolescence. Therefore, it is important that teachers talk about possibilities in tertiary education and where that education might lead.

Just because we presently have a better understanding of what is happening in the adolescent brain, that does not excuse their actions or allow parents or teachers to say, "What can you expect? It's all in the brain?" Teenagers need the best kind of teaching and modeling that we possess.

In the past, teachers have been told that they should watch for individual learning styles in students. They've been told that there are right brain learners, left brain learners, auditory learners, kinesthetic learners, visual learners, and so on. In fact, there are assessment tools for determining learning styles, and a great deal of money has been made marketing materials for teaching different learning styles. Recently, however, researchers tell us there is no credible evidence to support learning-style theories. Apparently, we all flip back and forth between ways of learning, depending on the context. What teachers need to do is to think about the clearest way to communicate what they are trying to do and to make it as engaging as possible.

In his book, *The Social Animal*, David Brooks describes a high school in which there is a strong emphasis on behavior and the way in which behavior influences thinking.

The Teenage Brain as a Work in Progress

The Academy started from the ground up. It taught its students to look at someone who was talking to them, how to sit up in class, how to nod to signal agreement, how to shake hands and say hello on first meeting . . . During the first weeks of school, they were taught how to walk down the hall, how to carry their books, how to say "Excuse me," if they bumped into one another. The teachers told them that, if they did the small stuff right, the big stuff would be much easier to master later on.[7]

If bad behavior has become habitual, then teachers can and should insist that the behavior change by telling the students they can "fake it until they make it." Good behavior becomes the habit, and forming such habits is one way to ensure that thinking is changed.

Students need to connect with teachers for them to make transitions necessary to do higher levels of thinking. Trust and empathy are needed, but it can be hard for the millennial generation to make connections with teachers in some situations. Gender, race, and socio-economic differences can stand in the way of connection.

Matt Silver, Ph.D., an award winning college professor who has coached students at a variety of ages, shares a technique that has worked for reaching different sorts of students.

Coaching in the Classroom by Matt Silvers, Ph.D. (University of Idaho), Professor of Health Sciences, named Professor of the Year, Outstanding Faculty in Teaching and Outstanding Faculty in Service at Eastern University, Cheney, Washington

During formative times in my professional development, I took advantage of several different coaching opportunities. At the time, I did not realize how impactful those experiences would be for me, or the ripple effect they would have on others' lives. Notably, I came to the realization that coaching is really just teaching in a different classroom.

In my first couple years as a college professor, I seemed to have forgotten this revelation. I *acted* like a teacher, which was not bad. However, I realized I had less interest in teaching and a perceived lower effectiveness in that role. So, I experimented with something new.

---

7. Brooks, *The Social Animal: The Hidden Sources of Love, Character, and Achievement*, 117.

I started thinking like a coach, treating my classes like teams, and coaching my students as if they were my athletes. A large component of this was the deliberate infusion of specific elements to which most students were already familiar. These included the development of individual and team 'season' goals for the semester, nicknames that reflected something unique about each student, and terminology changes. For instance, class sessions became "practice sessions," quizzes became "training drills" for exams (which were delivered on "game days"), and finals week became the "post-season" everyone trained for. Most importantly, I began connecting with my students similar to how a coach connects with his/her athletes. This allowed me to develop better relationships and rapport in ways that allowed me to challenge my students more.

This strategy has been a work in progress with elements added or stripped away depending on the situation. However, the theme and intent have worked well for me and my students. I certainly have to invest more time and thought, but due to the context imposed by the coaching theme, that time is more enjoyable and productive all around. My students seem to respond to, and appreciate, my care for them as a coach.

Obviously, certain personalities lend themselves to it better than others. Introverts are always tough nuts to crack, and extroverts have to be dialed back just a bit at times. I have not noticed a gender difference with this approach; both males and females seem to have responded well. If I were to venture a guess, I would think that high school males would respond well to this. It seems that in both high school and college, there can be a black and white difference in the intensity of engagement for males. At practice and during competition, they're "struttin' their stuff." In the classroom, they clam up. I have found that I can get them to open up a little more this way, so that they're not so much Jekyll and Hyde. This then helps me to reach them in other ways.

Discussion Questions

1. Given what we know about the way students learn, what do you think the defining characteristics of a good teacher are?

2. If it is true that behavior influences thinking, what actions do you see in students that might influence their thinking? How might those actions be changed to influence thinking in better ways?

3. Do students in your high school know about their own brain development? Are there ways in which you can bring them into discussion about their own learning?

4

Before Empathy

Tom: In our discussion about Nicholas Wolterstorff's educating for shalom model, we have been talking about how we develop empathy. I've also heard from a number of you concerns about some of the self-esteem emphasis we've focused on in the past. For this teacher training day we've invited Professor Patricia Bruininks to talk with us about justice, citizenship, and some groundwork we need to lay before students can be prepared to engage in empathy. Professor Bruininks graduated from Hope College, a Christian College in Holland, Michigan. She did her graduate work at the University of Oregon, and in her professional work she focuses on identifying and measuring the virtue of hope.

Patricia: Thank you for the invitation to talk with you today. I'm going to focus on Jesus' summary of the law and the prophets telling us to love the Lord with all of our hearts, soul, and mind and to love our neighbor as ourselves.

Thou Shalt Love Thy Self by Patricia Bruininks PhD

Justice and citizenship require looking outward from within. They are concerned with fairness and community, with others outside one's self. They require individuals to come together, relate with one another, and feel each other's joy and pain. In a word, they require love.

Love is a feeling, a desire, but most importantly, an action. Emotions come and go quickly, rarely lasting more than a few seconds. Moods last longer, for hours or even days[8]; but love, in order to truly be love, is constant. Once we come to love another person, we have chosen to think

---

8. Ekman, "Moods, Emotions, and Traits," 56–58.

about that person in a certain way, feel about that person in a certain way, and behave toward that person in a certain way. This "certain way" is not stagnate; its valence and magnitude fluctuate depending on circumstances surrounding that person's life and our own, but it is not temporary. We have made a commitment to see the other in this certain way with certain beliefs about his or her value that are central to the way we interact with this other.

What is this *certain way*? What does true love look like? First, it is non-consumptive.[9] We don't love others because of what they can do for us. I don't love my mother because she makes great pies, I don't love my husband because he does all of the yard work, and I don't love my children because they're smart. If these were the bases of love, it would be short-lived and sporadic like any other emotion. It would simply be a response to certain stimuli that in turn motivates behavior: a slice of apple pie leads to a hug, a beautifully landscaped yard deserves a steak dinner, and good grades are acknowledged with praise. Do something for me. I love you. I behave in a loving way towards you. That is not to say that kind acts don't warrant other kind acts in return, but this is not what I mean by love.

Second, love goes beyond the approval of others' existence; it is a desire for their well-being.[10] We are not simply satisfied with their presence; we want them to flourish. Homemade apple pie, a beautifully groomed lawn, and smart capable kids only matter if the baking, gardening, and studying are benefitting the doers. We desire others we love to experience enjoyment, growth, and self-efficacy through their actions.

We don't take delight in others only when they are producing and in turn flourishing. We experience pleasure simply in their existence.[11] Without them, we know our lives would be less interesting, less satisfying, and less meaningful. We take pleasure in them simply being there. If they were not there, I would be less than I am. The world would be less than it is. Whether they are presently flourishing or suffering, their presence is desired.

Love as a virtue must hold to the golden mean; too much or too little, and it turns into a vice.[12] Withholding love to manipulate others is not love. Showering others with excessive compliments and gifts is not love. Each of these misguided acts of love is conditional and is not concerned with

9. Taliaferro, "Love."
10. Taliaferro, "Love."
11. Taliaferro, "Love."
12. Taliaferro, "Love."

the well-being of the other. These acts are indicative of what C.S. Lewis describes as need-love, acting toward others in a way that will ensure you are loved in return.[13] If our attempts at this type of love don't produce the desired result, we may no longer appreciate pleasure in the other's existence and instead separate ourselves from him or her.

So how do we become the type of people who can experience this unconditional love for others? Not just for our parents, spouse, and children, but also acquaintances and strangers? Not just for people in our immediate community, but those in other cities, states, and on the other side of the globe? And how do we train our children to be citizens of their community, country, and world, and to be motivated to do justice because they love one another?

Before we can look outward toward others, we must look inward toward ourselves. This may sound counter-intuitive, but it's scriptural. In response to the Pharisees testing Jesus by asking him to state the most important religious law,

> Jesus replied: "Love the Lord your God with all your heart and with all your soul and with all your mind." This is the first and greatest commandment. And the second is like it: "Love your neighbor as yourself." Matthew 22: 37–39

The Greatest Commandment tells us that in addition to loving God, we must love others. And how are we to love others? As ourselves. If we do not exhibit virtuous love towards ourselves, how will we be able to do so toward others? A first reading of this commandment may lead us to see ourselves as the least important of these three, at the bottom of the hierarchy of love; but in order to live out this commandment, to obey and love God, we must start with ourselves.

Self-esteem

I can feel you bristling. For many of us parents and educators, we were taught to put ourselves last. Depending on your religious background, you may have experienced shame whenever you expressed a little self-love, such as pride at a job well done. For those in this camp (and I am one of them), we learned that we could never be good enough. The moment we felt any sense of self-satisfaction for mistakenly thinking that we had

---

13. Lewis, *The Four Loves*.

mastered some area of life, we were warned that we had better not get too big for our britches. These shame-inducing warnings may have been given out of a misguided understanding of love; perhaps our parents and teachers wanted us to continue to aspire for excellence, believing that self-pride might stop us in our tracks. They may have been trying to teach us that we are no more important than anyone else in hopes of creating in us a sense of duty to serve others. Instead we learned that self-deprecation was the best defense so that no one could accuse us of thinking too highly of ourselves. While this may have kept us in the good graces of others, it may have led to seeing ourselves as not worthy of love.

On the other hand, this concept of putting oneself last may seem foreign to younger generations. For many of our students, one focus of their early education has been to increase their self-esteem.[14] Self-esteem is essentially how you feel about your self-concept, and self-concept is how you answer the question, "Who am I?" Some schools have adopted self-esteem curricula that teach students they are capable and lovable, not dependent on who they are or what they do. Some schools include elevating this unconnected self-esteem as part of their mission statement. Students learn that they *should* feel good about themselves; to feel otherwise is *wrong*. The hope is that students with high self-esteem will perform better academically; however, research suggests that high self-esteem is more the by-product of doing well rather than the source of academic achievement.[15]

Feeling good about oneself sounds better than feeling bad; after all, aren't we all special in God's eyes? Doesn't God love us unconditionally? Yes, He does because we are spiritual creatures created by Him. God's hope is that we will discover and develop our gifts and talents in order to serve and, in turn, better understand God's unfailing love. The saying, "God loves you just the way you are, but He loves you too much for you to stay that way," comes to mind. This particular focus on self-esteem, which does not tap into our spiritual nature, says we should all feel great about ourselves no matter what we do or who we are. Consequently, this focus has had some unforeseen consequences.

Since educators are told that it is important for students to feel good about themselves, they may be hesitant to provide much needed critical feedback with the concern that students will interpret this feedback as negative and thus feel incapable. Grade inflation, the nemesis of educators, ensues.

---

14. Twenge, *Generation Me*.
15. Baumeister, et al., "Does High Self-esteem Cause Better Performance," 1–44.

High school students graduating in 2006 were twice as likely to report earning an A average in high school (fifteen percent) than those in 1976 (seven percent), and those who reported earning an A or A- average increased from around eighteen percent to thirty-two percent.[16] There has been more focus on being exceptional than challenging oneself to continue to improve in one's pursuits, and *exceptional* has slowly shifted toward *average*.

Second, we might think that encouraging high self-esteem (HSE) would be beneficial for students suffering from low self-esteem (LSE), but this idea is not supported by research. One study demonstrated that college students with LSE felt worse after telling themselves that they were lovable; those with already HSE felt slightly better.[17] The researchers surmised that repeating the phrase "I am lovable" led participants to think about their perceived worthiness, and those with LSE ended up focusing on all the ways in which they were not lovable. Another study examined the effect inflated praise had on eight to twelve-year-old children.[18] After drawing a picture, a "professional painter" gave the children inflated praise, non-inflated praise, or no praise. Afterwards, when given the opportunity to draw a more challenging picture, LSE children who had received inflated praise were less likely to take on the challenge while HSE children were more likely to do so. These types of attempts at helping people with low self-esteem only backfire, and this self-esteem curriculum may be ineffective or even harmful.

Third, how students feel about themselves has become separated from their self-concept. Students are taught they are *special* for no particular reason. They are *all* taught that they are special. Again, from a Christian point of view, there is some truth in this statement; but without being taught the difference between God's unconditional love and the "specialness" associated with discovering and developing one's strengths and talents, students may become more narcissistic.[19] They may exhibit an excessive interest in themselves or selfishness with a desire for admiration. Narcissists (think they) really love themselves; instead they have crossed over to the other side of the golden mean, making their self-love a vice. If those in the former

---

16. Twenge and Campbell, "Increases in Positive Self-views among High School Students," 1082–1086.

17. Wood et al., "Positive Self-statements: Power for Some, Peril for Others," 860–866.

18. Brummelman et al., "That's Not Just Beautiful–That's Incredibly Beautiful!" 728–735.

19. Twenge, *Generation Me*.

camp have developed the defense mechanism of self-deprecation, those in this camp have developed behaviors that ensure attention from others and rewards for just being themselves. Neither of these is indicative of self-love.

This leads to another consequence, which is an increased separation of oneself from others. If everyone has been told they are special, then everyone desires to be seen as above average. Since this is not mathematically possible, students may be more likely to engage in downward social comparison and self-enhancement in order to perceive themselves as better than average.[20] They are likely to focus on the others who are doing more poorly in academics or sports than they are while inflating their evaluation of their own abilities. They may disparage others' appearance as a way to boost their assessment of their own looks. Adolescence is a life stage when excessive energy is focused on self-evaluation, a phase the self-esteem movement has only magnified.

It is not hard to see how this has happened given our exceedingly individualistic culture. Individual achievement is seen as that, individual. Competition is seen as the best, if not the only, avenue for growth and excellence. This competition requires that we be better than others. Students are continually seeking justification for this high self-esteem that they are *supposed* to have, and seeking mastery for the sake of reward is one result. Another is underestimating or belittling the contributions of others. Self-concepts are also narrowed. How students describe themselves is more focused on their distinctiveness than their connectedness.[21] Ask an American student who she is, and she is more likely to say, "I'm an athlete," than, "I'm a daughter," or, "a friend." These individual selves grow further and further apart, fraying the threads that hold our communities together.

Few institutions foster competition, or at the very least self-judgment, better than the education system. Grades are assigned, awards are given, and accomplishments are displayed. Because we are so entrenched in this culture, it is difficult to see how else to motivate students to work hard and also love themselves even when they fail. Enter: self-compassion.

---

20. Neff, "Self-compassion, Self-esteem, and Well-being," 1–12.
21. Bochner, "Cross-cultural Differences in the Self Concept," 273–283.

Self-compassion

Compassion can be defined as agreeing to enter into others' suffering.[22] We don't simply pity others or express sympathy; we invite them to share the burden of their pain with us. By doing so, we become more aware of the situational variables causing their suffering. Our natural tendency is to over-attribute other persons' behavior or current circumstances to their personality or character and underestimate situational factors that may be in play. In fact, this tendency is so prevalent that it is referred to as the *fundamental attribution error*.[23] Compassion allows us to avoid this error by letting go of judgment so that we can simply *be* with the other in his or her suffering.

So goes self-compassion, except that now we are inviting ourselves to enter into our own suffering. That may sound counter-intuitive; after all, society frowns upon those who drown themselves in their own misery. This is not what I mean by entering into suffering; instead when we suffer, we are willing to recognize and sit with that suffering, and we more objectively assess the cause of that suffering. Instead of putting our energies toward feeling good about ourselves, we assess the situation for what it is.

According to Kristin Neff, self-compassion (SC) consists of three components: self-kindness, feelings of common humanity, and mindfulness.[24] The first, self-kindness, involves being understanding toward and patient with ourselves rather than harshly critical or dismissive. When we have failed, we accept the fact that we are not perfect. When our suffering is caused by outside circumstances, we take time to realize and acknowledge our pain instead of pretending to be okay. In a word, we allow ourselves to be vulnerable.

This vulnerability might seem like the very thing that would then spark all the self-protective thoughts and behaviors associated with self-esteem maintenance. The second aspect of SC, feelings of common humanity, protects us; seeing our self as part of humanity as opposed to a competitor in the human race levels the playing field and leaves us feeling less isolated. We *all* experience loss. We *all* make mistakes. We *all* fall short of our goals from time to time. Whose pain and feelings of isolation have

---

22. Nouwen et al., *Compassion: A Reflection on the Christian Life*.

23. Ross, "The Intuitive Psychologist and His Shortcomings: Distortions in the Attribution Process," 173–220.

24. Neff, "A Pilot Study and Randomized Controlled Trial of the Mindful Self-compassion Program."

not been lessened upon realizing that someone else has had the same negative experience or acted in the same horrible way to a loved one or failed at something important? Feeling excluded because of personal shortcomings only adds insult to injury. In fact, current research has demonstrated that emotional pain and physical pain are experienced similarly neurologically and somatically.[25] This emotional isolation, in turn, often leads to maladaptive behavior such as poor decision-making and unwarranted aggression.[26]

Third, when dealing with our own suffering, SC involves doing so mindfully instead of over-identifying with our failings or pain. Instead of responding to pain by focusing on the negative in our life (i.e., using words such as *always* and *never*), we take a more balanced view of the situation, seeing it for what it is in that moment.

We can see that striving for self-compassion is much more in accordance with the virtue of love than self-esteem. Self-esteem is consumptive; it is dependent upon our accomplishments or perceived accomplishments when no one has challenged us to do better. Self-compassion predicts more stable feelings of self-worth than self-esteem.[27] Self-compassion helps us to see our failings, not be overwhelmed by them, and strive to do better the next time which leads to a more stable assessment of ourselves.

Self-compassion also allows us to take pleasure in ourselves and to really like who we are, because it does not rely on competition. We realize that we are an important part of humanity, that without us the world would be a lesser place (think *It's a Wonderful Life*). And because we are viewing ourselves this way—and this is key—we are better able to view others in the same light. There is evidence that people high in self-compassion are better at perspective taking[28]; if we can give ourselves grace we can do the same for others. We can love others as ourselves.

In addition to being humans who are connected to one another, we are all children of God. As Henri Nouwen puts it, we are *beloved*.[29] This word beloved is relational in nature; in order to fully attain self-love, we must also recognize that someone else loves us unconditionally. Not only do we

---

25. MacDonald and Leary, "Why Does Social Exclusion Hurt? The Relationship between Social and Physical Pain," 202–223.

26. Williams and Nida, "Ostracism: Consequences and Coping," 71–75.

27. Neff and Vonk, "Self-compassion Versus Global Self-esteem: Two Different Ways of Relating to Oneself," 23–50.

28. Neff, "Self-compassion, Self-esteem, and Well-being," 1–12.

29. Nouwen, *Life of the Beloved*.

all screw up, but God loves us all despite our failings. When we succeed, he delights in our accomplishments. Reminding ourselves that we are not alone and that our self expands beyond our physical body and allows us to see others as beloved creatures who are neither all good nor all bad, and who deserve to be treated justly. Recognizing ourselves as connected to our creator and creation enables and motivates us to practice justice and be productive citizens of our communities.

Self-compassion in the Classroom

Self-compassion, like self-esteem, is associated with a number of positive traits such as a greater sense of well-being and life satisfaction and lower levels of depression. In addition it offers stronger protection against social comparison, public self-consciousness, self-rumination, anger, and close-mindedness than self-esteem.[30] These are good reasons in and of themselves to encourage self-compassion in the classroom. Teaching students to be kind to themselves and others, to see how they and others are connected, and to be mindful about their own and others' shortcomings is the real gold mine. Developing students' self-love will enable them to love others as they have been commanded, and this in turn will help them more fully realize God's love for his children. It is a beautiful, iterative process.

As with any psychological construct, there is variability in terms of the degree it is experienced by individuals. Adolescents and young adults who have experienced maternal support and positive family functioning tend to score higher on the Self-Compassion Scale (SCS) than those who have not.[31] Additionally, those who see themselves as experiencing life more uniquely (i.e., feeling that no one has the same thoughts or feelings as they do) score lower on the SCS. This relates to that feeling of isolation while not realizing that others experience the same hardships that we do.

Self-compassion may be strongly affected by how one was raised, but it can be increased through training. Kristin Neff and Christopher Germer have developed an 8-week Mindful Self-Compassion (MSC) training program. This program has been shown to increase levels of self-compassion, mindfulness, and well-being in a community sample with a mean age of

---

30. Neff and Vonk, "Self-compassion Versus Global Self-esteem: Two Different Ways of Relating to Oneself," 23–50.

31. Neff and McGehee, "Self-compassion and Psychological Resilience among Adolescents and Young Adults," 225–240.

fifty-one. These gains have been found at both 6-month and 1-year follow-ups, suggesting that participants continue to use tools that they learn in training long after the program is over.[32] Since the program's effectiveness has so far been found only with adults, we want to be careful about generalizing these findings to adolescents. These initial findings are encouraging, and educators may find inspiration from this program that can be incorporated into the classroom environment.

Psychological theories with implications for leading a virtuous life continue to be refined, as do all theories from all sciences; this is the nature of the scientific method. The hope of Christian psychologists, including this one, is that integrating this empirically derived understanding of how we do behave with a Christian worldview of how we should behave will lead us to more fully approximate God's love and the proper role we are to play in creation. Seeing ourselves through God's eyes will enable us to love ourselves, love others, and most importantly love God with all heart, soul, and mind.

Discussion Questions

1. How do we work on self-esteem in our community? In light of Professor Bruininks' comments, should we adjust our approach?
2. Are there ways in which we can develop self-compassion more fully in our students? How do they seem to be doing on this issue?
3. Do you agree that self-compassion is necessary in order to begin to love our neighbor? If so, how do we best communicate and model this?

---

32. Neff and Germer, "A Pilot Study and Randomized Controlled Trial of the Mindful Self-compassion Program."

5
Anatomy of a Judgment

Social studies teacher Brian Green *projected a picture onto the screen and asked, "What do you see?"*

Most of the students said they saw a young woman but a few of them said they saw a very old woman.

"Without pointing and using only words, tell what aspects of the picture make you see a very old woman," he instructed one of the students. Then he did the same asking about the young girl.

Projecting a second picture, Brian again asked the students what they saw.

Everyone said quickly, "That's the head of a horse."

"Did anyone see anything else?"

Finally, one boy who had said nothing earlier, said, "I can see a frog climbing down."

"Great," said Brian. "Now using only words, tell us what aspects of the picture help you see a frog."

After a few more pictures, Brian said, "We are going to be talking about two things that just happened here. First, when you state your opinion in this class, you must explain the basis on which you formed that opinion just as you did with these pictures. When we state an opinion or conclusion—whether it is about politics, science, art, or about justice and the rights of other—it must be made with an understanding of all of the factors that went into that opinion or judgment. The second is something you all will recognize but might not have noticed today. When we are in a group and the group is asked for an opinion, if one of us has an opinion that is different from the others, it is often very difficult to go against the crowd. An example of this occurred when only one of you perceived a frog in the picture the rest of you said was a horse. Jon bravely stood his ground and supported his opinion, but for many people that *is a difficult thing to do. It is especially difficult if the majority opinion is stated by people who are perceived as experts or leaders."*

For many Christians, religion is more a matter of the heart rather than a matter of the head. It is a matter of being born again, and telling others just how important that is. All of that is true; however, the response of a believer to a life in Christ means much more than a matter of the heart, and Christian high schools have a huge task in this regard. Sometimes it's complicated, though, because when teachers are faced with students who have been raised to believe that the Bible is the only authority, challenges can arise in the classroom. In these situations it can be helpful to show students that the themes of the Bible can shape our worldview in a way that can guide us more foundationally than quoting individual "proof-texts" from Scripture.

To help students develop a Christ-centered worldview, teachers have worked to create instructional units with a Creation-Fall-Redemption-Restoration (CFRR) motif.

- Creation: What is God's purpose for this aspect of creation that we are studying?
- Fall: How can we tell that as a result of sin this aspect of creation is not the way God wants it to be?
- Redemption: Because Jesus Christ came to save us, we can now work to make this part of creation more closely resemble how we believe God wants it to be. What plan can we make to do so?
- Restoration: How can we work together to carry out our plan to restore this aspect of creation?

Forming units around these questions works well whether the topics concern stewardship of the earth, living in communities, or examining actions studied in history or in literature. Teaching with the CFRR motif is one way teachers help students form the tendency to ask themselves the same kinds of questions about all of life; however, when used over and over, it becomes difficult to create such units in interesting, non-superficial ways so that students will be truly engaged in developing this tendency.

Part of the problem may occur when students are allowed to freely express opinions without providing supporting evidence based on research and on a careful study of the Bible. When teachers fail to demand in-depth research and readings about the topic and/or the biblical passages that inform the topic students see through the superficiality of the assignment.

This isn't easy, but we can learn from the work of others. For example, in his beautiful book *The Kids from Nowhere: The Story Behind the Arctic Educational Miracle*, George Guthridge describes teaching in-depth reading research to supposedly uneducable children of whale and walrus hunters on a blizzard-swept island in the Bering Sea.[33] As a middle and secondary school teacher of writing and literature, Guthridge is given the task of preparing the students for the statewide Future Problem-Solving Competition. With little training himself in problem-solving, with no idea whether there are problem-solving tools or techniques, and fully aware that his students don't even know what a term paper is, he begins with the phrase, "What because Why," meaning *what* problem is occurring and *why* that is a problem. For example, a village needs water but water is scarce. Getting water by drilling becomes the *what*, and the reason *why* it is a problem is because the permafrost makes drilling extremely more difficult and significant because of the high costs, frozen casings, and brackish water. Together the students became convinced that they would have to prove their findings, and the only way to do that would be by reading.

So, what does this have to do with Creation-Fall-Redemption-Restoration? If this is a serious way of studying, it must be combined with the steps that we know are part of problem solving.

1. Define and identify the problem
2. Analyze why this is a problem
3. Identify possible solutions to the problem in light of scientific and historical research along with an understanding of biblical teachings
4. Evaluate possible solutions
5. Select the best solution and present research on which the selection was based
6. Develop an action plan
7. Implement the action

Here is an example. Our city of Spokane, Washington, has hundreds of homeless teenagers on the streets at any given time. The exact number

---

33. Guthridge, *The Kids from Nowhere: The Story Behind the Arctic Educational Miracle*.

is difficult to assess because homelessness may be temporary depending on personal circumstances. Added to this is the fact that criminalization of the homeless increasingly occurs in ways such as making it illegal to sit, sleep, or place personal belongings in a public space. Most cities of the world have similar problems, including cities in countries that are welfare states.

If we are going to use the CFRR motif along with problem solving, we might lead the students through the following steps:

- *Creation:* What might be God's plan for the way people live? This involves a careful search of Scripture for passages concerning how people are to care for each other.

- *Fall:* Because of our fallen world, people are homeless and in need. Why are they homeless? What do they need? *Define* and *analyze* the problem. This involves a careful study of the various reasons for homelessness and the problems that exist for homeless teens in a particular community.

- *Redemption:* Because Jesus Christ suffered to redeem the world, it is now possible for us to work to alleviate the problems of the homeless. *Research* the needs of homeless teenagers. What is it that they most need? *Brainstorm* for possible solutions and research ways cities have attempted to help homeless teens. *Evaluate* the possible solutions and *Select* the best one using supporting evidence. *Develop an Action Plan* and explain why it should work. Possibly use Guthridge's "What Because Why" model; for example, "After careful study we believe that the Covenant House Program would be the best solution for Spokane's homeless teens because . . . "

- *Restoration:* In working at redeeming this part of our world until Christ returns, the students need to take the steps necessary to carry out their Action Plan. Actions are extremely important because our habits are formed more by our practices than by our thinking or speaking.

It is not possible nor is it even wise to attempt to teach every lesson or unit from a Creation-Fall-Redemption-Restoration motif, but it is often a fitting way to teach and can be a powerful way of showing the integration of biblical teachings with subject matter, encouraging students to ask, "How then shall we live?"

If we want our high school to be better, does that change the way we think about teaching and learning?

Change, according to Tom Vander Ark, formerly of the Gates Foundation, begins with criticizing or examining what you already have and hoping that your clientele sticks with you long enough to build something better. So, what are some questions a teaching staff might ask before they form a plan for change?

Here are suggestions:

- Is the organization of our school day, which we borrowed from a long tradition, really the best one for accomplishing our mission?
- Are we insisting that our students learn details about things that most adults know little about? Which facts and details are really important to remember?
- Do test scores adequately measure learning?

The *Cardus Phase I Facilitator's Guide* is a curriculum package for teachers and administrators that will help teachers and parents compare their own school's vision to the outcomes the school claims to produce. The end goal of a good high school education is a life-long ability to make careful judgments and thoughtful decisions that lead to deliberative actions in accordance with a biblical world-and-life view. We always teach with the ending goals in mind. That is true whether we are creating instructional units or planning the entire curriculum. Here are examples of things that two schools have worked on to achieve this kind of learning.

The goal of Lynden Christian High School in Washington is to help each student, as an image bearer of God, to discover and develop his or her individual worth, talents, gifts and responsibilities. The training of students incorporates every aspect of learning - the intellectual, the decisional, and the creative areas. Lynden Christian High School uses the LINKS notebook to guide their students' learning and reflection.

LINKS Notebook from Lynden Christian High School

The LINKS Notebook is a series of culminating assignments, aptitude tests, college and vocational tests, and (in some cases) projects.

First year students, apart from sections of their notebook designed to collect best efforts (academic and otherwise), write a Wellness Paper, an introspective essay written across the curriculum designed to answer the question, "*Who am I?*" Using various assessment tools in Biology, Bible, PE, and English, each student writes one paper on their physical, spiritual, emotional and social well-being. Their final project, the Wellness Paper, is a culmination of the four papers and encompasses a year's worth of introspection into one, comprehensive, colloquial essay.

Sophomores write the Career Paper, a research paper related to a field of interest designed to answer the question, "*What do I want to do?*" With the paper, students must present a five to six minute reflective presentation answering who they are and have been created to be, thus engendering contemplation and directing them toward a holistic understanding of their gifts as they relate to their future and their faith.

After identifying who they are in ninth grade and their interests in tenth grade, juniors begin to look beyond their high school career using different vehicles that will best get them thinking about their futures. This process includes a week long in-service from the career-counseling department in their Bible class in which they are presented with a myriad of choices. The Bible teacher then incorporates the lesson on *Calling*, with the idea of post-high choices. They are than asked to do a seven to eight minute presentation on calling, answering the question, "*How will I get there?*"

In their senior year, the students are now ready for the culminating presentation. They have collected four-years-worth of classroom projects, papers, tests scores, career choice data, and personal memories. Seniors are asked to reflect on their high school experience, challenging them to think about how they are being transformed into the kind of person God has called them to be—a caring and perceptive young adult who will transform this world for God's redemptive purposes. The seniors must answer, "*What am I going to do with the knowledge I now have?*" As mentors, staff encourage students to examine their identity in Christ, their interests as identified by their gifts, the paths that will enable them to best enhance that gift, and finally, how they intend to use their gifts for God's Kingdom.

Calvin Christian High School in Minneapolis links the aims of their school with evaluation conferences as well as with a final senior exhibition of learning.

The Aims of Calvin Christian High School are to enable students to:
- Experience faith as the foundation of personal identity, the source of calling to a life of service, and the impetus to life in community.

Teaching to Justice, Citizenship, and Civic Virtue

- Cultivate attitudes, habits, and skills that will allow them to flourish as individuals, as community members, and as Christ's servants in the wider world.
- Develop the knowledge and attitudes needed to assume their role as developers and stewards of the earth.
- Develop the knowledge and attitudes needed to participate in social and cultural development as Christians and to assume their role are agents of peace and justice.
- Develop the interests and abilities needed to read, view, and communicate effectively.
- Develop the interests, knowledge, and abilities to enjoy mathematical thinking and use it to serve every day and specialized purposes.
- Develop the interests, knowledge, and abilities to become engaged viewers, listeners, and participants in music, dance, theatre, and the fine arts.

These aims are reflected in an *Evaluation Conference*. Evaluation conferences are student-led. Students walk their parents through their portfolios with their advisors present to answer questions and provide context. At the end of the presentation, the students propose a list of learning goals for the coming semester. These are discussed by the student, the parents, and the advisor and accepted or revised as needed. Choices of independent project topics and experiential learning sites are usually discussed as a part of the goal setting process.

Senior Exhibition

During their last semester, students use their individual project time to prepare their senior exhibitions. Senior exhibitions include:

- An autobiography
- A plan for the future
- A portfolio of artifacts with written reflections demonstrating the students' competencies in relation to the aims of Calvin Christian High School
- A public exhibition of the product of a major project

Curriculum is often planned in such a way as to help students understand and become interested in work opportunities that are related to the topic.

Discussion Questions

1. Does our school have a culture of high expectations? How can we assess this?
2. Is teaching in our school focused on learning goals or simply on learning activities?
3. Do the parents of our students understand the importance of tertiary education?
4. What are the defining characteristics of a great high school? How would you rate our high school?
5. Do we have a "we expect success" attitude in our high school? How do we know?

Note: Part of chapter five first appeared in the Australian journal, *The Christian Teachers Journal*. March 2010, Vol. 18, No. 2. Published here with permission.

Intellectual Tenacity in the Christian Classroom by Janet Hauck, Librarian/University Archivist Whitworth University, Spokane, Washington

Every school in existence today is committed to teaching subject content to its students. Students attend classes, are given assignments, are tested, and are praised when their grades are high. All of this learning can be accomplished by any student with an intellectual gift or some good study skills, whether or not that student's heart is in the right place. It is a given that for some students learning comes easily, and for others, not so easily. Is there anything that teachers can do to encourage all students to excel? And, is this answer different for the teacher in a Christian school?

I would posit that the answer is definitely, "Yes, there is something different." A Christian school would typically add a second commitment to that of teaching subject content to its students. For example, the Christian university at which I work has as its motto: "An Education of Mind and Heart." The Christian high school attended by my children claims to be "Preparing Minds . . . Transforming Hearts." Obviously, a Christian school takes seriously the character content taught to its students, as well as the subject content. Here, the education of the mind and the education of the heart are intertwined in a unique way.

As a librarian at a Christian educational institution, I have pondered the connection between mind and heart for some time. In conversation with others, I have found that a common experience exists for librarians, in particular. This is the experience that most students, when faced with a research assignment, want to do just enough, but no more, than it takes to find sources to satisfy a teacher's minimum requirements. No matter how much we want students to go "above and beyond" in their work, it seems very hard for students to see the benefits of doing this.

Recently I have begun to think about this issue in terms of a virtue, especially an intellectual virtue. Phillip Dow writes about the virtue of "intellectual tenacity" in his book, *Virtuous Minds*, and I have taken it upon myself to build intellectual tenacity into my work with students. I start by talking with them about how one gets to be good at something, which elicits ideas of practice and perseverance. I then draw attention to the fact that one can apply these principles to intellectual pursuits, as well. This is where the mind and the heart intersect.

So, how can we encourage the virtue of intellectual tenacity in our students? In my case, I first teach them skills for doing effective research, making sure that my instruction is clear and compelling, and setting the students up to succeed. As they begin the research process, I help them evaluate the quality of their sources, making suggestions or pointing out gaps. But eventually there is a transfer of responsibility to the student; the teacher cannot do the students' research for them. It is here that the virtue of intellectual tenacity is brought to bear. If students persevere until the *best* sources are located, that is a skill that will last beyond the classroom.

Teachers that seek to educate students' hearts, as well as minds, are encouraging those under their care just as the Apostle Paul did with his Philippian converts. Paul wrote, "Brothers and sisters . . . Forgetting what is behind and straining toward what is ahead, I *press on* toward the goal to win the prize for which God has called me heavenward in Christ Jesus. All of us, then, who are mature should take such a view of things," Philippians 3:13–15 Students in a Christian school can grasp this concept. Pressing on and persevering in excellent research is a virtue that honors God.

6

A Theology of Citizenship

Tom Anderson: I know everyone has enjoyed getting to know our new teachers over the past few months, but I don't know if all of you have heard much about Joy's background. She's told you that she used to practice law and has studied politics. A number of years ago, she had a Fulbright grant to study in the Netherlands, and she focused on the work of Abraham Kuyper, a Dutch Calvinist who was both a preacher and a prime minister. I've asked her to talk with us little about a Christian perspective on citizenship.

Joy: Thanks, Tom. All of us are preparing citizens, and I've been giving some thought to what it means to be a Christian citizen. The comments I make here come from the work that I've been doing and speeches that I've given over the last few years to Christian communities across the nation.

Several years ago Charles and I, and our new son Matt, were in the Netherlands. Fulbright invited one student from each country to gather together for a few weeks to study the European Union and NATO. I represented the Netherlands, and a group of us gathered at a NATO dinner with some generals in Luxembourg.

It was 1992, and what used to be known as Yugoslavia had erupted into a series of wars, mass killings, and regional deportations. The world learned a new phrase as we started referring to this as *ethnic cleansing*. Americans were horrified by the mass killings that were reported on the news, and there was a lot of talk about whether the United States, NATO, or the United Nations should try playing a role.

At this lunch a small group sat with one of the generals and one person asked him, "Why can't we just go in there and stop the killing? We know what's right. We have the power. Evil is occurring; why can't we just stop it?"

The general looked at us, and in the sunlight the epaulets, stars, and bling on his shoulders and chest seemed to sparkle. Then he replied, "Well, there are two reasons. First, Americans have a low tolerance for seeing their children sent into war for countries we don't have much to do with. Second, it wouldn't work. This is ethnic strife. When ideologies clash, people fight to the death. You can't stop it with power; you need a different kind of solution."

A different kind of solution. The general was referring to a negotiated political arrangement in which people of different worldview perspectives could live together, sometimes referred to as political pluralism. The key for Christians is to consider questions like these:

- How are Christians to live with others in a fallen world?
- If you are a Christian, and you see evil in the world, what is your responsibility?
- Is there a Christian perspective on government, and if so, what sorts of wrongs should government be focused on?
- If we live in a community made up of people with different worldviews, should they be allowed to live according to their own beliefs even if we believe they are wrong? If we believe in pluralism or religious freedom, what happens if we believe that they are actually doing harm?

These are the questions that perplex Christians who think about public policy because they propose a fundamental challenge for those of us living as citizens in a global community made up of all kinds of different worldviews. It's a challenge for public policy makers, but it is also a challenge for every single one of us. Every one of us is a citizen, and every one of us impacts the community around us. We only have to look as far as the democratizing influence of technology in the Arab Spring movement or violence in the Middle East in part provoked by the American-made "Innocence of Muslims" film to see what kind of impact ordinary citizens can have.

As teachers it's our responsibility to help our students think through some of these very difficult questions. As a Christian, I have come to some conclusions, and this is the sort of framework that I'll be using with students and the community here. I am persuaded that Christian citizenship that emphasizes the rights of others to live and flourish in accordance with their own worldview is a necessary part of Christian witness in a broken but redeemed world.

A Theology of Citizenship

When Christians think about citizenship they often think about government and voting, but citizenship is bigger and broader than voting. Citizenship is the way that we live together and organize our lives together despite the differences between and among us. All of us have to ask ourselves, "Who is God in relationship to citizenship, and who are we to be in response to God?" What we need is a *theology of citizenship*.

A theology of citizenship, if it is truly going to be a theology, would need to start with who God is. We begin with a few things that we know for certain:

- As revealed by the Trinity, God is relational and created people to be relational as well. We are to be in solidarity with one another.[34]
- Both the Old and New Testaments tell us that God is glorified when communities and nations reflect God's will for justice, *shalom*, and care for the poor.
- God has shown a deep care for social issues and a deep anger towards injustice.
- We need to be careful that we do not argue for a works-righteousness approach to our work in the world. When we think of our obligations toward others, we remember that it is through God's grace that we know how to act in the world. We love because we have been loved. We show mercy because mercy has been shown to us. We do justice because of the justice we have experienced in God. Our obligation toward others springs from the joy and beauty that is found in Christ.

As I have been thinking about this, I've drawn from the work of a theologian who is about my age. In the early 1990s, Croatian Miroslav Volf was facing the terror that the Serbs were inflicting on his community. As a Christian, he was experiencing tension between what he believed to be his obligation to embrace the other, and his own resentment about being excluded in society.

Volf was born in Croatia but moved to what is now Serbia when he was a child. His father was a Pentecostal minister in a country framed by Marxism and hostile to religious belief. The family was monitored by government officials, and Volf was the only openly Christian student in his schools. He was asking this question, "As Christians, who do we need to be to live in harmony with others?"

---

34. I am indebted to Matthew Kaemingk for reminding me to begin with these points.

Teaching to Justice, Citizenship, and Civic Virtue

As Volf developed his thinking over his professional career, first at Fuller Theological Seminary and now at Yale, he observed that with respect to public life Christians have engaged culture in two damaging ways. Some withdraw from public life focusing only on church, and others get engaged in public life but they do so in a way that coerces others. In his recent book *A Public Faith: How Followers of Christ Should Serve the Common Good*, Volf concludes that one group is following a "secular exclusion" of religion from public life and the other is engaged in "religious totalitarianism." He articulates a third way arguing that in a world where many worldviews live together we should develop "religious exclusivism but political pluralism."[35]

Volf is not the first to call for this. He has drawn, over the years, from the theology and intellectual gifts of many including Nicholas Wolterstorff, Richard Mouw, Steve Monsma, Alvin and Neal Plantinga, and others. What is so interesting to me is that he has come to this conclusion as both a Christian and as a victim of perpetrators. He says it is the only practical way to protect room for truth claims among faiths. It seems to me that we must take this seriously.

God created us with the ability to engage in political community, and this engagement carries not just rights but obligations. This means that we have a responsibility to think through the institutional process necessary to achieve justice for everyone—a justice that allows people to also pursue the other non-political callings for which we were created. When we consider Creation, Fall, Redemption, and Restoration, we see that God through Christ helps us renew all of our responsibilities on earth including the responsibility to govern. While we live in a fallen but redeemed world, just governments will provide laws that treat everyone equally. Christian politics means that Christian citizens "without any public privilege, will seek to live at peace with all people and will work to build states and an international order to promote justice for everyone."[36]

The responsibility of government is to protect a healthy public commons in which the long term health and well-being of all people is recognized. Public justice should be the guiding principle for our laws, and public justice calls for both institutional and confessional pluralism.

Institutional pluralism draws from a Reformed theological concept of sphere sovereignty to demonstrate that in public life there are many different ways in which we engage the world. We are family members. We

---

35. Volf, *A Public Faith: How Followers of Christ Should Serve the Common Good*.
36. Center for Public Justice, "Guidelines."

worship. We can be entrepreneurs. It is important to remember that the institutions that support these activities have different responsibilities. A church is not a family, a family is not a business, and a government is not a church. Our responsibility is to think through the different callings of these different institutions. Human flourishing can occur only when there is room in society for people to function in all the different capacities that God has called them to.

Confessional pluralism means that while we live in a broken world we recognize that people have to have room to live according to the worldview they feel called to. For Christians thinking about citizenship, the important question is, "What sorts of responsibilities do governments have toward people of other worldviews and faith traditions?"

The biblical foundation for this kind of pluralism is centered in three different places. First, the Old Testament is filled with directives from the prophets that demonstrate civil authorities have a responsibility to the poor, the sick, and the weak. The books of Micah and Amos are replete with commands to do justice and to let justice roll down like a river. Isaiah 65 describes for us what a good city should look like: the people are healthy and live to an old age, conflict is handled and peace reigns, the vineyards yield fruit, and people will not labor in vain but will enjoy their labor and live in houses that they build. Justice is connected to healthy, flourishing communities.

Second, Christ's life demonstrates that the Kingdom of God is not to be brought about by the sword. Christ used stories, persuasion, and encouragement to demonstrate what our lives should be in this world. Political pluralism is a tool that protects other institutions as they engage in other kinds of persuasive work. The church has room to be what the church is called to be. Families and businesses have room to flourish in the way that they are called. There is room to share the love of Christ and to act in accordance with the way Christ calls us to live, but there is not room to coerce others to do the same.

Third, in the parable of the wheat and tares found in Matthew 13, Christ shows us that it is not our job to separate the wheat from the weeds. In this parable, the farmer's workers asked if they should pull out the weeds from the fields. The farmer said no, so the sun and the rain fell equally on the wheat and the weeds until the harvest. Political pluralism allows public, legal justice to fall equally on everyone in society even if we consider that some of the people are weeds.

The question then is, how do we actually do it?

I have found that conversations about the most difficult tensions between us—the rights of the gay community, rights of the undocumented, and the role of faith in public school—occur more easily across lines of difference when we have three things going for us:

- We know the other side
- We have a philosophy about the other that allows the other to flourish
- We see what we have in common

With these three, we see a need for a theological grounding for what shapes our civil understanding of the room for ourselves and for others to live in accordance with our deepest conviction and worldview. We then need to know the other in order to figure out how this public, political room will manifest.

What then does this mean for us? The harder job is figuring out what this means in politics. For us, I'd say that as teachers we have more room to encourage students to ask questions without necessarily having to frame all of the answers. I think this is where we begin to emphasize *empathy*. I am not sure all that this entails, but I am sure that we can begin to do some important work.

Sometimes developing empathy can mean demonstrating that there are different perspectives that have good evidence behind each of them. The website www.procon.org is so helpful in showing all of us how to think about a wide variety of issues that challenge thoughtful citizens—immigration, healthcare, legalization of marijuana, religious freedom, the death penalty, taxes, and so forth.

In this day and age it is easier and easier to hear from those who are not like us, which really helps us develop empathy. There is no better film series than *Eyes on the Prize* for thinking about race and justice because we hear from the very people that were instrumental in working for racial justice in our own country. Films like *Miss Representation* and *Inequality for All* are among the hundreds of documentaries on Netflix that help us think about gender and economic injustice.

I know many of you have ideas about how to teach to justice and citizenship in the classroom. I'm looking forward to learning from all of you and wishing there were some sort of clearinghouse where we could share and steal ideas!

Discussion Questions

1. How does your school community think about citizenship?
2. In what ways do you encourage students to develop empathy or to see things from another person's perspective?

7

Engaging Culture—History, Politics and Technology

DAVE: LAST NIGHT MY son was home from college with his girlfriend. Our social justice-oriented daughter was talking about President Obama and healthcare when the girlfriend said, 'You don't mean you support him, do you? You can't be a Christian and a Democrat!' My daughter was gearing up for a fight, but my son kicked her under the table. It made me laugh, Joy. I tried to talk about your pluralism idea, but sadly we all just got confused.

Joy: I know. Maybe pluralism is a hard concept to grasp, but I think if we start with empathy and learning about others we are on the way to getting it.

The *Cardus Educational Survey* demonstrated that Protestant Christian School graduates are avoiding political action and report a surprisingly low interest in politics altogether when compared with Catholic school graduates. This might be unfortunate; but we find that though "politics" can be off-putting for many Christians because it is perceived as nasty, many people of faith are nonetheless committed to making a difference in the world. If we broaden our understanding of politics to the concept of "citizenship," then we have a framework in which to encourage engagement with the world.

In the following conversation a high school principal and faculty who teach first-year students at Whitworth University, a Christian college, talk with the Midland teachers about how they help students engage with culture.

Tom: I'd like to introduce our panelists for today's in-service discussion. Dale Soden is a history professor and author of *The Reverend Mark Matthews: An*

Engaging Culture—History, Politics and Technology

Activist in the Progressive Era. He did his graduate work at the University of Washington and focuses on American intellectual history through the eyes of faith. Kathryn Lee, a political science professor, did her graduate work at Johns Hopkins University. She also attended law school and clerked for the Washington State Supreme Court after working with the U.S. Department of Justice. Kevin Huinink is a principal at Niagara Association for Christian Education in Canada. He focuses on the issue of technology.

Joe: I love history, and I'm really interested to hear Dale talk a little about his work.

Dale: Teaching history at almost any level presents a great opportunity to have students explore issues related to faith and/or virtues. Perhaps most accessible as well as, in my opinion, most important is the virtue of empathy. Scripture is clear that we are commanded to love our neighbor as ourselves, yet we often assume that the ability to love another human being is something that comes naturally or is simply an act of will. I don't believe that is the case. Love is difficult, and love requires practice. One of the most important elements in the effort to practice love is the ability to see the world through the eyes of another. In a simple sense, this is the act of empathy. Good historical thinking virtually requires one to be able to empathize with figures in the past. This sounds so simple and yet, after teaching at the college-level for over thirty years, I have found it to be profoundly difficult.

Joe: Can you give some examples?

Dale: Well, if one is teaching the American Civil War, it is necessary to try and see the world through the eyes of a variety of individuals and/or groups – Northern abolitionists, Southern slaveholders, enslaved Africans, West Point-trained generals, poor white farmers, draft resisters, grieving mothers etc. All of this can take a tremendous bout of emotional energy as well as intellectual skill. The results can be both challenging and frustrating, but they can also be rewarding in the sense that it generally encourages a deep sense of humility.

In my History of the Vietnam War course, I try to raise difficult questions regarding the My Lai Massacre. When historians try to understand why such horrible things can occur, it requires a careful examination of the circumstances and the personalities of people involved. It is not easy to understand with certainty what was going through the minds of William Calley, Ernest Medina, Paul Meadlo, and a host of others from Charlie Company. In class, we try to at least account for the way in which they were trained, the horrible experiences of the weeks leading up to My Lai, and the orders that were given by commanding officers.

At the same time, we also try to comprehend the savagery of the event itself. I ask students after that whether they feel any degree of empathy with the soldiers from Charlie Company. I ask those who are Christians to consider whether there is any room for empathy, compassion, or love for the perpetrators, or whether Christianity calls us simply to evaluate on the basis of a standard of justice or moral right or wrong. I don't try to impose an easy answer, but I suggest that as a Christian one must try to do both but always with a profound sense of humility. Can any of them honestly say that they would not have gone along with what others were doing? Can they be certain that in those circumstances they would not have been caught up in a frenzy of violence; and if so how would they want to be judged, and secondly how should they be judged? Are there any times when they have found themselves simply going along with the "crowd" because it was the easy thing to do?

Andrea: But aren't you teaching them that morality is relative?

Dale: Not really. I guess I want students to be more guarded about their own moral compass and how easy it is to not do the "right" thing even if one is a Christian.

A second opportunity for teachers of history is to help students explore the human condition. History can teach us remarkable examples of courage and persistence against tremendous social and political forces. It can also teach us about the nature of pride, ignorance, greed, and selfishness. Good history teachers help students understand how complex human behavior is and how difficult it is to do what's good even when we think we know what's good.

The challenging part is to help students develop a keener eye for those moments in which we should exercise a kind of moral judgment on actors or eras in the past. From the practice of slavery to the mass executions in Stalinist Russia or Pol Pot's Cambodia, history's judgment on the moral failure of past people and cultures is often clear. At other points that judgment is less clear whether that be on the legacy of a John D. Rockefeller, a Lyndon Johnson, or an Emma Goldman. Studying history should lead to a certain spirit of both intellectual and moral humility. We see through a glass dimly. We are hardly aware of our own limitations, biases, and prejudices. History should teach us to be cautious about our own certitudes and convictions as well as reinforce for us some of our deepest convictions.

Engaging Culture—History, Politics and Technology

Joe: Why did you get into this field?

Dale: It is a remarkable privilege to be able to carry forward the stories of the past. It is a remarkable privilege and a source of great power to be able to influence the narrative of the past. Christian historians should carry this privilege lightly, but not shrink from the opportunity it presents to help students think deeply about some of the most important ideas and events that mark the human race.

As for my own work, I have tried principally to find stories of individuals and groups who seem significantly motivated by religious principles and values to try and make the Pacific Northwest, and/or the world, a better place. I have wanted to make a small contribution to how we understand the Pacific Northwest by pointing to the many examples, generally unknown to most people, who tried to shape public policy, work for social justice, or shape the broader culture in some form. These have ranged from individual clergy and groups such as the Woman's Christian Temperance Union who early on fought against domestic violence, to African American pastors, Catholic priests, and Protestant ministers who fought for civil rights in Washington and Oregon.

Joy: Since all of you know how interested I am in politics, can we hear from Kathy on how she teaches Christians to think about government?

Kathy: Christians should care about government because it is an institution established by God to create conditions for human flourishing. It is the only institution that possesses legitimate force in a democratic society, and, therefore, it can wield power to make people safe as well as to secure public or collective goods. A police force wields power so that citizens can be safe. Through its taxation power, a government can provide roads, bridges, Medicare and public education; public goods without which a society could not flourish. Government contributes to the common good; Christians should be engaged in working for the common good.

Joy: What do you think it means to be a Christian citizen?

Kathy: To be a Christian citizen means that I recognize that government is an institution that has the power to affect people's lives in both a positive and negative way; and, therefore, if I am to love my neighbor, I should be somewhat informed about issues involved at all levels of government. I should also participate, at the very least, by voting on a regular basis. Not all Christians have the time or interest to be what I might call "servant-activists," but Christian citizens at the very least should vote, thereby acknowledging that they are part of a civil society. A Christian citizen should also be humble because Christians do not have a corner on the truth; to quote I Corinthians 13, "now we see through a glass darkly." In addition to being humble, Christian citizens should not use angry rhetoric nor caricature those who think differently than they do. Participation in politics for Christians includes not just taking positions on policy issues, but also being thoughtful about how we talk about those positions.

Joy: What do you think about party politics? Should Christians be Democrats or Republicans?

Kathy: Whether or not to be a partisan advocate, that is, whether to identify with a particular party, is a difficult question to answer because, as a Christian, my first allegiance is to the kingdom of God, not to a country or to a party. Consequently, a Christian should constantly be aware that no political party perfectly reflects God's will or God's truth. But the American system of government organizes itself through parties, so, for example, congressional committees are chaired by members of the party that controls the two chambers, and we vote for candidates who align with parties. If Christians are going to have impact within the governmental structure, then they must align with a party, rather than standing on the sidelines. One can say that he or she is an independent, but typically elections are partisan. If one is going to run for office or work for someone in public office, one has to align with a party. Christians certainly can have impact by lobbying public officials through organizations such as Focus on the Family or Christians for Comprehensive Immigration Reform; but it is just as important for some Christians to be on the inside of government, and parties are the path to that position.

Dave: I told our group that my son's girlfriend was visiting and we had a family talk about politics the other night. One of the things she said is that the poor will always be with us so Democrats are on the wrong path to emphasize the welfare state. What do you think?

Kathy: The statement, "the poor will always be with us," simply states a fact of life; inequalities will always be with us in a fallen world. The statement does not mean that Christians as individuals or governments should do nothing to help the poor. The Old Testament prophets spoke of justice, a *shalom* justice, that includes paying attention to the material conditions of people's lives. Old Testament scholar Perry Yoder, for example, writes that in the Hebrew Scriptures it is clear that justice is "the grounding of God's rule" and that "justice is part of who God is." He says that God's rule in the world is a justice which benefits the weak and oppressed and moves against the powerful. Perry cites Psalm 146 as an example of a biblical text that supports an emphasis on justice: "[W]ho executes justice for the oppressed; who gives food to the hungry; The Lord sets the prisoners free; the Lord opens the eyes of the blind. The Lord lifts up those who are bowed down; the Lord loves the righteous. The Lord watches over the strangers; he upholds the orphan and the widow, but the way of the wicked he brings to ruin." Yoder suggests that the justice in the Bible is *shalom* justice, a justice that restores people to a state of well-being; and the concept of salvation encompasses more than salvation from sin, a fact reflected in the message of Matthew 25.

Andrea: One of the things we talk about in terms of the mission of the school is whether we should be focusing on saving others or on working in the world. What thoughts do you have on that?

Kathy: I think for educators, as opposed to the church, it is more important to be concerned about politics in this world than the salvation of others. I think God knows about an individual's relationship with Him in a way that I cannot. What I can do is affect people's lives here and now through working for justice and peace through politics. One of my favorite statements is attributed to St. Francis: "Preach the Gospel at all times and when necessary use words." I think preaching the Gospel includes being involved in government and politics to achieve justice.

Dave: As a Christian, what kind of news sources do you look at?

Kathy: I think newspapers (and their websites) such as the *New York Times*, *The Christian Science Monitor*, and the *Wall Street Journal* are sources Christians should consider when seeking information about events both here and abroad. Magazines that have a particular political position and are well respected include *The Atlantic*, *Harper's*, *First Things*, *National Review*, and *Weekly Standard*. Christians should be wary of sources that do not attempt at all to be tempered in their approach to politics. A liberal example of this phenomenon would be dailykos.com; a conservative example would be redstate.com.

One of the most disturbing developments in American mainstream media is the decreasing number of journalists covering events abroad. Christians should be interested in world events, so I would suggest seeking out information from the websites of the BBC and Al Jazeera, places where world events are often covered in more depth than in the American mainstream media.

At this point Kevin Huinink joined the conversation by Skype.

Joe: Kevin describes himself as husband, dad, teacher, student, coach, runner, singer, lover of life and was recommended to us as someone who is thoughtful about the use of technology in schools. Kevin, what would you say are the benefits of new developments in technology?

Kevin: Technology, no matter what it is, will eventually find its way into our lives, and into education. Like anything else, it will bring both benefits and challenges.

Technology is always employed to make something easier for humanity. It takes something that was once done manually or with toil and makes it more accessible, easier to accomplish, require less effort, save time, or create more output with less input. Tools are fantastic, God-given gifts; and an answer to the cultural mandate: to fill, subdue, and rule the earth.

Technology has made our lives richer, easier, and for the most part, better. Think back just twenty years in the areas of transportation, medicine, power, communication, and information. No one could have predicted the things we are capable of or take for granted today.

Advances in communication and information technology have had the largest impacts on education. Where research used to involve a trip to the local library, students are now able to quickly search on almost any topic through access to the Internet or online research databases. Quality information is available much more quickly, and students are able to collaborate online pulling together and publishing what they have learned in a matter of hours rather than weeks. Where students once had limited access to printed information or were relegated to photocopying resources for their use, they now have access to continuously available digital copies, many searchable by keyword.

Online publishing and collaboration has allowed teachers to communicate and share items more easily with students in new ways and formats and has increased access to education for students who once found it a challenge to learn in traditional classroom environments.

Andrea: What concerns you about the use of technology?

Kevin: Our reliance on technology has ushered in new ways of thinking and doing things. Fundamentally it has changed the way we learn, along with some of the attitudes we have toward studying and education. Along with the access to information and ability to communicate much more easily comes complacency toward needing to exercise our brains in specific ways. What used to be accepted as necessary to memorize is now at our fingertips as quickly as a search query.

Concerns around how technology is changing how we learn are as old as the invention of the book. Just as the book was once suspected to make learning too easy as one could just refer to the printed copy, we continue to face the challenge of knowing what is of value to learn. What is unique about our current day and age is the pace at which technology is developing. New technologies emerge almost more quickly than we know how to effectively use them. With the novelty of our new tools and toys, we can lose sight of the very goals of our teaching and learning as we attempt to adopt and figure out new mediums.

Perhaps of greatest concern and aside from academic interests, young people are quick to adopt new technologies without positive role models or guidelines for their use. While it may be healthy for young people to have their own space free from adults, we have seen how poorly used technology without boundaries, convention, or rules results in hurt, bullying, and impulsive behavior. Understandably technologies become less 'cool' once their parents and teachers have adopted them; but new technologies and social spaces continue to emerge, and unsupervised experimentation continues to lead to misuse and dangerous outcomes. As they are by definition places for young people, this has made schools a main place for these types of activities affecting social development and experiences as well as school culture.

Joy: How might teachers in other content areas make better use of technology in their classrooms?

Kevin: The challenges technology presents to teachers and students seem to stay the same. Students as digital natives are generally comfortable using technology, and teachers as digital immigrants are not. While one might argue that our newest and youngest teachers are now digital natives, the pace of technology will continue to place students and teachers in different spheres of experience. This does not, however, remove the teacher as the resident expert with respect to the substance of the subject of study.

Technology has the potential to bridge the divide if the teacher is willing to consider its use and application in their subject area and in their classes. This does come with its own set of challenges and fears as students may be more comfortable with using technology than the teacher, or as technology continues to change and develop. It will require some change, discomfort, and work. The outcomes, however, can open up new and exciting ways of learning. Students are far more ignorant of technological application than many of us think or fear. The teacher's job in their subject area is to bring about substance to the medium and depth to the technology.

Two of the best ways to begin are to reach out to colleagues in your own subject area who are employing technology in their classrooms. Collegial collaboration can set a teacher in the right direction and allow him or her to learn from others' experiences and mistakes. The second is to be willing to play and experiment with the technology. While it may seem on the surface to be frivolous activity or without productive ends, a teacher who has dabbled in and is familiar with technology is far more effective in communicating with students about its use.

Dave: What do you think about students having digital devices or computers at school or in classrooms?

Kevin: As time progresses, digital devices will become more and more intertwined with our daily lives; and students' lives are no exception. While one might argue that use of personal digital or electronic devices at the elementary level has limited benefit, at the secondary level their use can hardly be avoided. From writing papers, researching, crafting presentations, to collaboration with fellow students the use of computers in the classroom can be a very helpful and welcome addition. As each device has multiple uses and functions from word processor and browser to phone, music player, and communication device, their use is also a potential distraction from the learning that needs to occur.

We need to remember that digital devices are not magic, nor do they need to exist in a category on their own apart from any other materials a student may bring to the classroom. Students should be held accountable for passing notes in class with respect to the distraction itself and the content of the message. The same should be true of communicating digitally. The text of today is the same as the note of yesteryear and doesn't need a new policy to control it. Playing games or distracted browsing on a device is no different than the same on a piece of paper, reading a book or comic, or doing anything else in class.

Depending on the teacher's level of comfort, anything brought into the classroom should be either put away or put to use in service of learning. If a student needs to take notes, they should do that with their device. If the class would like to fact check or look further into a topic, the teacher should feel free to ask a student to research something online with their device quickly for use in discussion. If it helps to share notes or resources between teacher, students, or classmates, the technology should make that easier and more accessible. Listening to music during teacher directed time is obviously off limits, but use of a music player as a tool to focus while working has assisted many students in the often more busy classrooms we find today.

Brian: So what is a teacher to do about technology?

Kevin: At least three things. First, play with it and become familiar. Second, be where your students are and help them figure it out. Third, be prepared for technology in your classroom both the kind you bring and the rest that will inevitably show up.

Kathy: Thanks, Kevin. I have conflicting thoughts about technology in the classroom. I use very little in my classroom which might be a function of age to be honest, but I am concerned that students remain active and engaged in their learning. Use of new technology, like use of YouTube clips in Power Point slides, can keep attention, especially when attention spans are shorter and shorter. That said, I have had students express appreciation that I don't use PowerPoint slides in a way that simply repeats material in a textbook but instead emphasize discussion of common readings. My major concern is to avoid passive learning which, I think, does not produce active and critical thinkers.

Joy: You've mentioned YouTube clips. What are your thoughts about films and DVDs in class?

Kathy: When it comes to television shows and movies, I employ two rules of thumb to guide my use of them: A) is the violence gratuitous to the point that it overwhelms the narrative? And B) are certain groups of people objectified and/or ridiculed? I think too much gratuitous violence and objectification of women in particular has the potential to desensitize us to the dignity individuals have because they are made in God's image.

Hollywood, like any other sector of our economy, reflects the effects of the flawed human condition. I think that the horrible tragedy in Bangladesh, in which more than 1,100 garment factory workers (mostly women) died, also reflects the fact that the marketplace is flawed. Sex and violence sells as do inexpensive clothes. Greed and the exploitation it prompts explain much of human suffering. To criticize Hollywood without criticizing other sectors of our economy for exploiting humans rings hollow.

Joy: In my graduate work, we engaged with college students who were trying to think about political life through the eyes of faith. I wanted to share some of these opinion pieces with you all so you can see how thoughtful young people can be and how much we can learn from them even when these issues seem to be so convoluted. We might not agree with each of these writers, but we can admire the way they work to consider policy and faith together.

> **Spreading Genetically Modified Opportunities** by Kevin Gleim, college student
>
> Developing countries must increase agricultural production by fifty percent in the next twenty-five years in order to meet food demands. In addition, one fifth of all people in developing countries, equating to roughly 828 million, suffer from chronic malnourishment. Though controversial in most developed countries, the use of genetically modified organisms (GMOs) is imperative to developing countries that are faced with widespread starvation.
>
> There is little solid evidence to suggest that GMOs are dangerous to human health or the environment in the near future. Thus, Christians concerned with food security around the world would do well to consider the use of GMOs as a method to combat famine.
>
> Most people do not realize that genetic engineering has been occurring for over ten thousand years through artificial selection and hybridization.
>
> These practices continued until 1973 when two scientists innovatively developed a technique to take a DNA fragment from one organism, copy it, and insert it into other organisms – controlling the expression of traits.
>
> By the 1980s, large biotechnology corporations were beginning to patent products they manufactured. Over the course of the next few decades the divide between the European Union's and the United States' policies regarding GMOs widened, inadvertently thrusting developing countries into the middle of this burgeoning debate. By 1997, the EU instated mandatory labeling on all genetically modified food products.
>
> The US offered food aid in the midst of the 2002 Southeast African food crisis, but Zambia and Zimbabwe rejected the crops due to the potential of genetic contamination and the loss of valuable European export markets.
>
> This precautionary approach is a default avoidant stance that can be taken when encountering risk. However, since most arguments about the short-term risks associated with GMOs are laced with hypothetical terminology and lack scientific certainty, cautious consumers are left fearing unknown consequences that may never be realized.

Therefore, GMOs should not be banned because they are able to serve as a resourceful short-term solution to world hunger if the abuse of power by corporations and cautious consumer-driven countries is repressed. The benefits of GMO food production outweigh the risks of genetic engineering because of this pivotal opportunity to feed thousands of starving people.

Nonetheless, we must not ignore these negative effects, but rather change the institutions that cause them in order to lay the foundation for an infrastructure that incorporates GMOs.

Crops can be modified to be resistant to herbicides, pests, diseases, drought, and high salt content in the ground. This is enormously beneficial to developing countries because it vastly increases the efficiency of their agricultural practices and allows for adaptation to poor soil conditions. However, the primary method to obtain GMOs is through biotechnology corporations.

I would argue that the business model of biotechnology companies traps farmers in a system of economic dependence. Companies patent their seeds and genetically engineer them to be sterile, causing farmers to return every year for new expensive seeds and herbicide. These patent rights are then abused when seeds blow into neighboring non-GMO fields and the company then sues the farmer for "stealing" their product. Biotechnology companies also pour a great deal of money into campaigns to prevent mandatory labeling on GMOs.

This abuse of power by biotechnology corporations prevents developing countries from obtaining GMOs and perpetuates the political impasse between the US and EU. Should this technology reach the people in developing countries who need it most, they will be given the opportunity to become autonomous from all political and economic constraints.

Since corporations have historically controlled the use of biotechnology and since the precautionary approach of some nations hurts starving populations, non-governmental organizations (NGOs) must assist in changing the structure that encourages the use of GMOs.

Due to the political constraints from the EU, NGOs must encourage governments in developing countries to grow genetically engineered crops. Once this is accomplished, NGOs must obtain the biotechnology to grow GMOs through research since corporations won't be willing to give up products that generate excessive revenue and because these countries lack the infrastructure to finance large research initiatives. This is a daunting task, but a Christian response on this issue demands support for ethical pro-GMO NGOs and activism against the unjust corporations that exploit the customers of their products. In order to rebuild this structure, Christians must work to strengthen civil society so that we are able to compassionately reach out to those less fortunate than ourselves. It is not the role of the government to ban GMOs, but rather to facilitate their development in developing countries crippled by famine. When this occurs, developing countries will have the autonomy to implement the use of GMOs in their developmental structure and terminate widespread starvation.

The Most Exciting Gift this Holiday Season? You Guessed it: Water
by Kristina Grossman, college student

Do the most good this season—Give gifts that impact lives, really.

There are thousands of gifts we could give our friends and family this Christmas. But many Americans utilize the opportunities from non-profit organizations to give a gift that gives back to someone in need. This popular mode of "alternative giving," such as buying animals, medicine, hand-made crafts, and child sponsorships are great ways to give in the name of a loved one, and give back simultaneously. Although, how do we select from the many choices? World Vision, Heifer International, and Compassion International are some of the great non-profits to choose from. But what will help the most people, be the most cost-effective gift, and also the most sustainable method of development? If we're going to give "alternatively," should we not do it the best way possible?

The clear answer (pun intended) is: water. Unsafe water sources are the leading cause of death in the world. Over 780 million people lack clean water. Bringing clean water is argued as the one of the best ways to help raise someone out of poverty. Notably, it's the poorest of people that lack the things Americans take for granted most. We turn on faucets multiple times a day without even thinking of it as harmful. Unclean water can affect everything. Water security can be the holistic answer. When overall health is improved, and time is not spent retrieving water, educational and entrepreneurial opportunities are then available. It helps the most vulnerable: women, children, and the sick—the trickle-down effect of water security is vast, and can end the cycle of poverty.

Reduction of poverty occurs through both public and private efforts. The United States has given foreign aid to sub-Saharan Africa, the region in the world most affected by water insecurity, for decades. On average $425 million is given by the United States Agency for International Development to water-related aid. But over 40 percent of sub-Saharan Africans still live without access to a safe drinking water source. Along with the government, private aid can go a long way is specifically targeting water insecurity issues in states.

As Christians we are called to give to the people that need it the most. But how is this possible with the incredible need? Economics professor Bruce Wydick polled sixteen development economists in *Christianity Today* article, "Cost-Effective Compassion: The 10 Most Popular Strategies for Helping the Poor," to rate the "most common poverty intervention to which ordinary people donate their money, in terms of impact and cost-effectiveness per donated dollar."[37] The number one rated option was clean water to rural villages; therefore, this "cheap-plus-effective" option is an "endearing combination."

Support of water security projects may not have the appeal of child sponsorship because it is less individualized and personal. But, giving toward water projects is showing good stewardship and a smart and compassionate attitude. In Matthew 25:40, Jesus says, "Whatever you did for one of the least of these . . . you did for me." Our actions reflect our deepest nature, and in the spirit of celebrating Jesus, the greatest gift, we must not give what may seem the "most exciting" to us, but something that can show love the best way possible. This Christmas let's empower people, and get back to the origin of giving.

> *Charity: Water* and *Blood: Water Mission* are two non-profits organizations to support that are making excellent strides in water security.

37. Wydick, "Cost-Effective Compassion: The 10 Most Popular Strategies for Helping the Poor," 24.

Drones, Faith and Complicated Decision-making by Nathan Reid, college student

For the past decade, American presidents have relied heavily upon drone-launched missiles to strike terrorists. These strikes have mainly taken place in Pakistan and Yemen, and have come at an undesirable price. In October, Amnesty International and Human Rights Watch claimed that more than eighty-seven civilians had been killed in the ten drone attacks that they had been able to research, which represents a fraction of the total drone strikes launched by the United States. The United Nations investigator assigned to civilian deaths from military strikes estimated that at least 400 civilians have been killed in the past decade by American drone strikes. These two reports are not only startling, but have many Americans crying out for more transparency from the CIA and the military's Joint Special Operations Command.

While the United States' drone program has had success in preventing terrorist attacks on Americans, the program is shrouded in darkness and secrecy. Amnesty International raises an important question: How do drone operators know for sure that they can avoid civilian casualties, with the "near certainty" qualification that is required by President Obama? Additional questions to consider are: How do these operators know if a suspected militant on the ground is an "imminent and continuing threat" to the United States? Is the unintended killing of civilian bystanders creating more new militants that join terrorist groups than these attacks are eliminating?

As drone technology advances we have to ask whether the United States is turning more decision making in these terrorist assassinations to the intelligence of a semi-autonomous machine without a human controlling it? Many of the attacks on suspected Al Qaeda or Taliban figures are "signature strikes," and rely on electronic surveillance that detects patterns of behaviors instead of real-time human judgment by the operator or those on the ground. The most common approach is the OODA Loop, or the ability of a human or machine to observe, orient, decide and act, keeping itself "in the loop" of necessary information to make choices. But even this formulation is limited. When does the drones' technology advance to the point where the human factor is completely removed, and the drone is able to fire a missile on its own?

The concern about autonomous drones does not imply that humans alone would handle all situations flawlessly. Consider the 1988 downing of an Iranian civilian airliner by a Navy ship, which mistook it for a fighter jet. Would a drone, emotionally unaffected by the situation have misinterpreted a climbing commercial aircraft for an attacking fighter jet? Would a drone, with no self-confidence that it had leapt to the correct conclusion without considering all the facts, have overlooked sending a warning signal to the aircraft on both military and civilian communication channels?

As Christians, how are we supposed to respond to these new advancements in technology? Larry May's book *War Crimes and Just War* highlights a famous case: if soldier A has an enemy soldier, B, in his sights and soldier B is naked taking a bath hundreds of yard behind the front lines, and is unarmed and is oblivious to the fact that he is vulnerable, would soldier A be wrong to take the shot? A military drone would take the shot without hesitation if the target fits certain criteria; however, if it is a human behind the controls, the human can consider what it means to be humane or just, something that a drone has no capability of knowing.

It would seem that the drones and humans working together could augment the weaknesses of either working alone. Drones collect the facts without bias and humans provide judgment when the decision-making requires more than executing an algorithm. Humans provide the ethical thinking, adaptability, and critical reasoning, as well as empathy for those who might become collateral damage in these strikes. These traits of intelligence do not lie in the increasingly complex algorithms of computer programs. Christians have to ask some deeper questions before we blindly accept the benefits of technology.

The Little Engine That Couldn't: Against Increased Coal Train Traffic by Oliva Godt, college student

Coal still provides a large amount of energy in the United States. In 2005, it accounted for 27.8 percent of the nation's usage. Each person, on average, consumes about twenty pounds of coal per day. While coal may be a cheap source of energy, it is also one of the dirtiest. Between mining, transportation, and burning it emits some of the highest levels of CO_2. In Spokane, coal is at the heart of an intense debate. Coal companies are looking to export some of the US's vast coal resources to developing nations like China and India. To do this, they must transport coal from central states to Pacific ports. But first, coal trains must pass through Spokane. Increasing coal traffic has both clear economic benefits (more jobs, increased revenue from exports) and environmental concerns. Weighing these sides, I suggest blocking increased coal train traffic in Spokane.

After creation and then the fall, all relationships were broken. Often, we focus on sin cutting off our personal relationship with God, but the scope is, in my opinion, much larger than that. Healthy relationships among people were broken, the relationship with our self was broken, and humanity's relationship with creation was also broken. Evidence of these broken relationships is everywhere. Broken relationships between humans cause societal injustices like racism, sexism, and hatred. A broken relationship between humanity and creation is also evident. Recently, NASA released a study saying that 97 percent of climate scientists agree that humans have likely caused global climate change.[38] In science lingo, 97 percent is a startlingly large number. Scientists never agree in that high of a percentage. Moreover, deforestation, extinction of animal species, and widespread pollution are further evidence of an unhealthy relationship between nature and humanity.

This realization is profoundly humbling. Taking on this posture—posture of humility—is a necessary step in reevaluating how we interact with God's creation. Humans have and will continue to mess up. It's a reality of the fallen world we live in. This 'messing up' extends beyond just interaction between people, but to our interaction with nature as well. While this picture looks bleak, we have the encouraging call to bring God's kingdom to earth today (Matthew 6:10). We are charged with working toward total reconciliation of these relationships, including reconciliation with God's good earth.

The Bible is full of clues displaying a healthy relationship between humanity and creation. Often times, Christians quote Genesis 1:28. It states that humans should 'subdue' the earth. Unfortunately, this verse

---

38. NASA, "Consensus: 97% of Climate Scientists Agree."

has often been misconstrued to suggest that we can do anything to the earth that we want. However, Genesis 2:15 states that man should "take care" of creation, counterbalancing this seemingly clear green light to use creation at will. While the creation narrative affirms that humanity has a special role in nature, it rejects the claim that humans can do whatever they may want to it. Instead, a healthy human-nature relationship is one filled with love. Part of loving well includes observing, diagnosing, and healing. Thanks to modern science, we have the ability to diagnose the earth's overall health. According to many climate scientists, the earth is very sick. How, then, can we act out of love and reconciliation upon hearing this news?

If God has left us to care for creation, I suggest we seriously consider the profound environmental impacts of coal trains. As mentioned, coal is one of the biggest polluters. It emits high levels of CO_2, a leading cause of human induced global climate change. By taking a stand against increased coal train traffic through Spokane, we have the opportunity to not only protect ourselves from local pollution but to also decrease global pollution. As a Christian woman committed to healing all broken relationships, including the one between humanity and nature, I suggest the decreased use of coal trains.

I understand that this stance has economic implications. Undoubtedly, increased coal exports would boost our economy. However, I cannot ignore environmental warning signs. With global climate change such a pressing issue, and coal so clearly a large contributor, it would seem irresponsible to increase coal exports. Instead, I suggest decreasing coal dependence in favor of cleaner energy technologies. Although this may not be as cost-effective initially, in the long run, it will be more sustainable. Our good earth is very ill, and if we are its caretakers, it only makes sense to remove those practices which are harming it. While this will not be an easy change, I am confident that humble, creative individuals will be able to propose solutions which treat God's creation with integrity and love.

For more information, visit:

Beyond Coal Washington: http://content.sierraclub.org/coal/washington

Restoring Eden: http://restoringeden.org/

8
Engaging Culture—Dealing with Difference

Tom: This month our conversation with university faculty continues, and we are going to focus on difference. We'll look mostly at race but also touch briefly on how Christian communities can think well about gender and sexual identity. I've invited some Christian university faculty to engage with us. Larry Burnley is an assistant vice president for diversity and intercultural studies and also a professor of history. His graduate work, a PhD and an MDiv, was at the University of Pennsylvania. Esther Louie was an assistant dean for intercultural student affairs. She has worked for the Act Six Leadership & Scholarship Initiative which connects urban ministries and faith-based colleges in order to equip emerging urban leaders to provide transformative leadership for the university campus and their communities at home. Mark Killian is a sociologist who did his graduate work at the University of Cincinnati. He specializes in urban and religious social environments, and before becoming a sociologist he taught high school at a Christian school in Ohio. Stacy Keogh graduated from George Fox University, a Christian college outside of Portland, Oregon. She did her graduate work in sociology at the University of New Mexico and focuses on peace movements and political sociology. Finally, Kathy Lee is joining us again. I introduced Kathy last month, and I asked her to return today because she teaches classes on gender, justice and difference through the eyes of faith.

Andrea: I'm interested in what you all think about issues like race, gender, and poverty. Do you think that with an African American president our country is now a post-racial society?

Mark: The interplay between race and class is complex, leading to contentious debates between highly respected scholars. In his award winning book, *The Declining Significance of Race*, William Julius Wilson makes the claim that class statuses have a greater effect on the plight of African Americans than all forms of racism. In response, Douglas Massey and Nancy Denton argue in *American Apartheid*, that racism, in particular racial segregation, remains the primary cause of the disadvantaged state of African Americans and, by extension, other non-dominant racial and ethnic groups. Citing the inequitable differences of housing values between segregated Caucasian and African American *middle class* neighborhoods, Massey and Denton demonstrate that racism is still prevalent in American society.

Joy: Tom told us that you used to be a high school teacher—is that right?

Mark: Yes, I loved teaching high school, but I was also interested in doing some other kinds of work as well. Anecdotally, I witnessed racial segregation first-hand as a high school teacher. After teaching social studies at a suburban Christian Academy for seven years, I transitioned to teaching at an inner city public Montessori high school. Unlike the overwhelmingly Caucasian population of the Christian Academy, the Montessori school offered explicit engagements with individuals of various races and ethnicities. Moreover, given the nature of Montessori curriculum, racial and ethnic inclusion and integration were of primary importance. That is, until lunch time, when students would sit at segregated tables.

Joy: Do you know why that was? Did you ever ask them?

Mark: My inquiry into lunchroom segregation revealed that, typically, students eat with individuals they know from their bus. Of course bussing reflects neighborhood racial and ethnic compositions. As a consequence, I came to discover that racial and ethnic differences are often not a product of individuals' choices, such as choosing not to sit with students of other races and ethnicities at lunch due to prejudice, rather these differences are inscribed in our geography and, even more so, in our institutions, such as high schools. Thus, I do not believe we live in a post-racial society, but, as Eduardo Bonilla-Siva argues in his book, *Racism Without Racists*, a society whose social structure facilitates the privilege of Caucasians and the disadvantages of non-dominant racial and ethnic groups.

Larry: I am also among those who strongly disagree with persons who claim that we now find ourselves living in a "post-racial" period in our nation's history. In fact, I'm of the opinion that W. E. B. Du Bois' prophetic assertion in 1903 that "The problem of the twentieth century is the problem of the color line," was sadly short-sighted.[39] As we gather here in the twenty

---

39. Du Bois, *The Souls of Black Folk*, 9.

first century, "race" may not be the problem, but race and racism—both individual and structural forms—are without question alive and well.

Examples of the persistent significance, relevance, and impact associated with the social construction of *race* can be seen in a variety of ways. These include, but are not limited to, the following: the persistent disproportional racial gaps between whites and people of color in areas of families and children living in poverty; employment; household income; low infant birth weight; infant mortality; judicial system and prison population composition; prison sentencing; death penalty decisions; academic achievement; high school graduation and dropout rates; high school suspension and expulsion; college/university retention and graduation; and the persistent marginalization and exclusion of scholarly voices, lenses, and topics of examination in core (required) reading in K-20 education in the U.S.

These disparities/outcomes are shaped, informed, and, in many cases, sustained by historical racialized policies and practices that were and continue to have as their primary goal the reproduction of the privileged positions of power enjoyed by persons and communities that are inextricably tied to white (racial), male, abled (physical and cognitive), and straight identities. These are just some examples of how race continues to be a significant and relevant issue that any God-loving person who cares about justice should pay attention to.

Dave: That sounds like theory, which interests me. Can you help us think about how high school curriculum can take this into consideration? What should we be thinking about?

Larry: Regarding race and education, I'd say that required curriculum of educational institutions in the U.S.—private, public, secular, and faith-based—perpetuates, reinforces, and advances false notions of the supremacy of European culture, whiteness (read "race"), maleness, and other privileged identities. Conversely, identities associated with indigenous populations of color, women and others have and continue to be distorted, marginalized and/or excluded in *required* reading in K-20 education in the U.S.

Andrea: Are you talking about racist groups?

Larry: No, my use of the term "white supremacy or superiority" is not intended to reference violent or segregationist groups such as Aryan Nation or the Ku Klux Klan. I acknowledge the racist ideological orientation and violent histories of these groups and others like them, but my comments are not directed at them, at least not primarily. What I mean by "white supremacy" is the theory or belief, conscious and unconscious, that

Engaging Culture—Dealing with Difference

white people and by extension their culture and their history are innately "ordained by God" or, as a result of "natural selection," superior to people of other races.

Dave: I want to understand what you are saying, but at the same time I have to admit that I am feeling kind of defensive. Can you give us an example?

Larry: One clear example is the manner in which western Christian orthodoxy associates "goodness and superiority" of whiteness in virtually every dimension of the human experience. The church perpetuates this. Just think about the iconic presentation of Jesus. Even Jesus is white, and this is so strange. At a time when religious scholars are supposed to be committed to the highest standards of academic rigor and objectivity there remains a persistent, contradictory, and even hypocritical silence among far too many scholars when it comes to presenting a more historically accurate racial/ethnic representation of the Son of God; a first century Jew living in Palestine. Even as we talk together, untold thousands are flocking to movie theatres around the world to expose themselves to "proof" that God is indeed a white man.

Andrea: What do you mean?

Larry: Just think about the message of films like *Son of God*, or Mel Gibson's *The Passion of the Christ*. God and Jesus are white. So, do we live in a post-racial society? Absolutely not! Should Christians still pay attention to or care about race? If we are concerned with and committed to a life that "honors God, follows Christ, and serves and is served by humanity," the answer must be a resounding, "Yes!"

Esther: Some of you are looking a little uncomfortable. Let me add to this conversation. I think that life is so complex and confusing some days that we want to simplify, to delete, to reshuffle, to forget, or to just make life easier for ourselves. We start to throw out what seems to be "not important." And that includes those moments or those thoughts that trouble, stress, and bother us. We find ourselves saying, "If you would just let that be, if you would just not rock the boat, if you would not bring up these issues, if you would not keep emphasizing these touchy, stress-filled points, can we just forget about that?" Race or ethnicity, gender, sexual orientation, religion, faith, and spirituality often fall into this category of "let's not bring that up" or "let's not talk about that." These core values of identity have never been well explained to us, nor did we learn how to handle our and other's in a positive manner anywhere along our life's lessons. In fact, we learned from the time when we were children that we were not to notice or say things about others nor was this process of what we notice or not notice ever explained—why there are fat people, skinny people, people that have darker skin or lighter skin, different hair (good hair, bad hair), girls who dressed and acted like boys, boys who played with dolls, or people who attended other churches, synagogues, or temples.

Andrea: Do you think we live in a post-racial society?

Esther: No. Furthermore, we have not developed positive images, thoughts, or even respectful or accurate vocabulary to speak about our differences. In school, especially in the early years, we learned how to bully by saying unkind things to the kids were different; and by everyone's silence, we were affirmed in making fun of those kids who were different. Even in college, the process for understanding, learning, or recognizing differences between and amongst us may be intellectualized in academic courses; but we are not taught how to be functional or competent on a daily interactive or engaging way with those we perceive as different. How we approach a person face-to-face who may be different from us in their race, ethnicity, culture, sexual orientation, or religion/faith/spirituality—we really do not know quite how we can or should interact with them with respect, appropriateness and even with curiosity. Our natural inclination is to find those with whom we can identify with in all of these categories and stay in the ease of familiarity. We continue to stay in our safe groups rarely venturing forth to bridge across to those who may appear different from us.

People have said to me, "Do we have to talk about our differences? Can't we just get along and accept that we're all human? You highlight the problems by always focusing on how we're different; can't we just move on?" I've been told by my friends, "I don't see you as a Chinese woman. I just see you as Esther." In their need to simplify their tensions and stress (in my interpretation, let's only talk about what makes them comfortable), they deny who I am and my primary identity. When we deny the other's race/ethnicity, sexual orientation, gender, and faith/religion/spirituality by saying that it does not matter in so many different ways, we deny their humanity, their person-hood. Further, when we refuse to accept that inequality exists in our society, we deny privilege to those who are different (intentional or unintentional), and we deny that we may be oppressing people because of their race/ethnicity, gender, sexual orientation, or faith/religion/spirituality.

Stacy: As a sociologist I agree that we have to pay attention to these issues. Christians are called to live intentional lifestyles that model the

Engaging Culture—Dealing with Difference

perfect life of Christ. That means that we have to be aware of the struggles that face us in everyday life. However, this task can be hindered by personal conflicts in our own lives. Many individuals, Christian or otherwise, struggle to understand their own racial, gender, and sexual identity. We should care about gender, race, sexual identity because we all have these identities! How can we begin to heal the world if we, ourselves, feel lost and confused? Moreover, how can we (Christians) help others without putting ourselves in another's shoes? We must learn to recognize the conflicting social messages we receive that make us confused about our place in the world. We have to learn to recognize those messages, and realize they affect others differently. That is a lot of work, but that is our calling as Christians: to be truly intentional in our relationship with Christ and with others.

Andrea: What do you think about feminism? Are there any issues that you think high school students face or fail to deal with well so that it challenges them when they come to college?

Stacy: In my opinion, feminism is about achieving equal rights, privileges, and equal social respectability regardless of gender. That doesn't mean "women acting like men." It means, women being appreciated for who they are. It means men being appreciated for who they are. It means not requiring men and women to fit into boxes that society has prescribed for them. God has not made us exactly the same, nor are we just two groups of people. And, God didn't make mistakes, either. The Bible says we are "fearfully and wonderfully made" (Psalm 139) in a number of ways.

Unfortunately, our societal influences are difficult to recognize until we are trained to think critically. Some of that is formal training, but most of it, I think, is just reaching a level of experience, maturity, and adulthood that is difficult to reach as a teenager.

Joy: I've heard that many Christians are starting to argue that the Bible is ambiguous about the sexual relationships between people of the same gender. What would you say to parents who think that feminism or conversations about sexual identity are threats to Christian worldview?

Stacy: Parents' concerns about these conversations are rooted in arguments that are valid. Those conversations can be scary and even threatening to some; however, understanding the historical context and the social issues of the day may shed light on some of those concerns. Not all Christian communities delve into that type of material in a Bible study class.

I would also say, in addition to becoming more educated about the context in which those statements were written, that Christ called us to love one another, not to condemn.

These conversations are indeed difficult, but the reality is these issues are very prevalent in our everyday world. We have to recognize that so we know how to deal with particular situations when they inevitably cross our paths.

Kathy: Whenever communities say they are going to talk about diversity, I imagine eyes rolling and the unspoken thought, "Not again," going through someone's mind. Diversity, pluralism, and difference are all are concepts which twenty-first century America talks about a lot, particularly in universities. My workplace is a Christian university, and, to its credit, it requires students to take courses in American diversity and global perspectives. This is not political correctness. This is not a nod to the latest higher education fad. This is, instead, recognition that society is structured in such a way that not all identities are treated justly and some are discriminated against based on identity. Part of being a Christian in the world is to acknowledge injustice and to do something about it.

Esther: I love this quote by Edward T. Hall, "One of the many paths of enlightenment is the discovery of ourselves, and this can be achieved whenever one truly knows others who are different." How could Christians not pay attention to the core of identity for ourselves and for others? How could we not be concerned with our own personal, professional, community, and spiritual growth and that of others? The primary identity factors of gender, race and ethnicity, and gender and sexual orientation (social constructions as they are in our western society), truly cannot be ignored. Our faith/religion/spirituality or lack of a belief system is also a core identity component for many in our world; to ignore or down play the importance of who we are, and how we chose to engage with the difference found in others has impacted our past, present and future through wars, slavery and treatment of women. To not examine these important identity concepts would be to choose to stay ignorant on what inspires, motivates, encourages, and supports our daily lives. How and what we teach our children, our students, and ourselves about who we are and what makes us tick seems critical if we are to survive well.

Dave: Do you think race or poverty is a bigger issue in society today?

Larry: I don't think one is "bigger" than the other. I believe poverty is created, produced, and sustained by human greed and consumption. It is

Engaging Culture—Dealing with Difference

constructed. Race and poverty intersect, and I would say both get manipulated so some people or groups can stay in power. In some ways, race and poverty exist in dialectic relationship with one another. This point has been made by a number of scholars, clergy, and activists. But, I think Dr. King was most eloquent in demonstrating the relationship of race and poverty in his 1967 address, "Beyond Vietnam." He said, in part:

> Since I am a preacher by calling, I suppose it is not surprising that I have seven major reasons for bringing Vietnam into the field of my moral vision. There is at the outset a very obvious and almost facile connection between the war in Vietnam and the struggle I and others have been waging in America. A few years ago there was a shining moment in that struggle. It seemed as if there was a real promise of hope for the poor, both black and white, through the poverty program. There were experiments, hopes, new beginnings. Then came the buildup in Vietnam, and I watched this program broken and eviscerated as if it were some idle political plaything of a society gone mad on war. And I knew that America would never invest the necessary funds or energies in rehabilitation of its poor so long as adventures like Vietnam continued to draw men and skills and money like some demonic, destructive suction tube. So I was increasingly compelled to see the war as an enemy of the poor and to attack it as such.
>
> Perhaps a more tragic recognition of reality took place when it became clear to me that the war was doing far more than devastating the hopes of the poor at home. It was sending their sons and their brothers and their husbands to fight and to die in extraordinarily high proportions relative to the rest of the population. We were taking the black young men who had been crippled by our society and sending them eight thousand miles away to guarantee liberties in Southeast Asia which they had not found in southwest Georgia and East Harlem. So we have been repeatedly faced with the cruel irony of watching Negro and white boys on TV screens as they kill and die together for a nation that has been unable to seat them together in the same schools. So we watch them in brutal solidarity burning the huts of a poor village, but we realize that they would hardly live on the same block in Chicago. I could not be silent in the face of such cruel manipulation of the poor.[40]

Kathy: Why should Christians care about injustices based on identity? I think there are both biblical and theological reasons for caring. I was raised

---

40. King, Jr., "Beyond Vietnam."

in the Reformed tradition which emphasized that persons are created in God's image. Theologians over the centuries have struggled to define what that exactly means. Does it mean that as God's image-bearers we have certain capacities? That we have a certain role in creation? As I have read more about the theology of disabilities, I have been reminded that all don't possess capacities that we might think of as image-bearers such as reason and creativity. Nicholas Wolterstorff has written that when Christians discuss being made in God's image they often are talking about having a nature that is like God's and/or having capacities. But, what about those we refer to as disabled? How do we answer the question, "What does it mean to be made in God's image?" The question itself suggests that we in our humanity are tied to God in a significant manner such that we have worth.

Another reason Christians should care about these identities is that God cares about injustice. In his book, *Journey Toward Justice*, Wolterstorff points out that while Scripture does not lay out a theory of justice, it does speak about acting justly. In the Old Testament, one sees "the preferential option for the vulnerable," meaning particular care for widows, sojourners, and fatherless. Being a widow, a sojourner, and an orphan were identities that might provoke unjust treatment.

The New Testament continues this theme, especially in the life of Jesus, who in Matthew 25 underscores that love means caring for those on the margins. Loving someone means you do that which will advance her flourishing and respect her worth.

I think that the primary reason Christians should care is that God loves us all no matter our identity. That may seem simplistic; but, in the end, I find this the most compelling reason. This love is demonstrated in Jesus's interaction with those who were on the margins, and whose identity prompted discrimination, e.g., women, lepers.

Some might assert that race and gender are no longer issues. Some point to the fact that Hillary Clinton almost achieved the Democratic nomination in 2008 and that Sarah Palin was the Republican vice presidential nominee as evidence that women have achieved parity. Still others point to the election of President Obama as evidence that we live in a post-racial society. But, the wage gap between men and women persists and the "glass ceiling" still exists such that women face challenges in breaking into upper management positions. Single mothers continue to face challenges to support and care for their children. On the fiftieth anniversary of Dr. Martin Luther King's "I Have a Dream" speech, economic disparities between blacks and whites persist. In 2011, almost 27 percent of black households were in poverty which was nearly triple the 9 percent white rate according to the Census Bureau.

The existence of racism in the criminal justice system can be demonstrated in varying sentences given to black and white defendants who committed the same crime and the imposition of the death penalty. One need only read Michelle Alexander's book, *The New Jim Crow: Mass Incarceration in the Age of Colorblindness*, to realize that the criminal justice system must be a focus of lawmakers and citizens alike in this country if we hope to have a just and fair system.

Andrea: We've talked a lot about race and a little about gender. Is there anything you'd encourage us to be thinking about regarding sexual identity?

Kathy: Of the three identities—gender, race and sexual identity—the last remains the most fraught in the Christian community. Others have addressed the fact that one can still affirm the Bible as authoritative, yet interpret key passages in a different way regarding sexual orientation. (See Matthew Vines, *God and the Gay Christian: The Biblical Support for Same-Sex Relationships* and James V. Brownson, *Bible, Gender, Sexuality: Reframing the Church's Debate on Same-Sex Relationships*.) As a Christian, I am called to honor a person's dignity and to provide a place where he or she can be authentic.

Discriminating on the basis of sexual identity denies a person his or her dignity and requires him or her to be inauthentic. Churches can still maintain their beliefs regarding sexual orientation; however, as a fellow citizen and a citizen who happens to be Christian, I think I must work for an individual's dignity and for a place where that person can be his or her true self. Doing so honors God's image-bearer.

Discussion Questions

1. What work does your school community do on the issue of difference? Would you say parents and students embrace difference, or are they challenged by it?
2. Do you see a dominant political perspective in your students? Do you think those in the minority feel comfortable expressing their beliefs, or does your school avoid discussion of politics?

9
Engaging Culture—the Arts and Business

Joy: One of my friends teaching in the mid-west told me that she wanted to direct the show *The Laramie Project* at her high school. That's the play about Matthew Shepard who was killed in Wyoming. Since Matthew Shepard was gay, the parents objected to the play. She wasn't able to do it. How do you think our community would react to that? The play is about the trial and what happens after his body is found. It's a docudrama about something that really happened.

Joe: I don't know. It's hard to say because a lot of people are really afraid of anything to do with sexuality.

Tom Anderson: This month we have another group of college faculty here to talk with us about faith and the arts and business. We won't be able to engage in conversation with them, but each will give a short talk by Skype and then we can discuss these matters on our own later. Please welcome Diana Trotter, Ben Brody, and Craig Hinnenkamp.

Diana Trotter is a theatre professor at Whitworth University and did her graduate work at the University of California, Berkeley. She received the Association for American Community Theatre's national award for Best Production and Best Director for *Lonely Planet* (1999). Diana, how do you choose plays for your production season?

Diana: When I'm considering plays for production at Whitworth, or anywhere I'm asked to direct for that matter, I am guided by three sources: the Bible, the needs of the community, and my gut. Let me briefly consider each of these:

Engaging Culture—the Arts and Business

The Bible

When I cite the Bible as one of my guiding sources, I don't mean that a play has to have a certain message, be overtly "Christian," or even promote a particular point of view. I use the Bible as a guide because it contains within it the entire spectrum of human experience. Every conceivable emotion, every type of character, practically every possible situation can be found in the pages of the Old and New Testaments. Lust, greed, envy, and fear exist alongside love, courage, hope and joy. There are wars, plagues and famines, stories of betrayal, sin, and loss. Likewise, those same pages are filled with miracles, angelic visitations, creation and rebirth, and countless images of God and His great love for humanity. The stories encompass characters from every walk of life—the most exalted King and the lowliest servant, tax collectors and prostitutes, priests and farmers, soldiers and spies, widows and orphans. The Bible also points to the abundance of artistic forms and styles as well with its inclusion of history, politics, poetry, prophetic visions and story. When I study the immense breadth and depth of Scripture, I find that the selection of plays and performances that can be considered "biblical" is vast indeed.

Does that mean I will produce absolutely anything? No, it doesn't. For me, the key aspect of what I see in the Bible is the possibility of redemption. No matter how gruesome the stories or how wicked the characters, ultimately the Bible points to grace even if the pointing consists of demonstrating how desperately we need it. That doesn't mean plays and stories have to have a happy ending. Grace, love, and redemption are deep, rich concepts, and simple yet complex at the same time. As the Gospel story teaches us, they may not always be readily apparent and in fact may come at a terrible cost.

Needs of the community

I believe theatre should always be an integral part of its community. My particular community includes the students with which I work, the Whitworth University population, and the larger community in which Whitworth resides. Because I direct theatre as part of the university academic program, one of my principle responsibilities is to provide a range of educational opportunities for the theatre students. Our stage is our laboratory, and the productions are training grounds for the students who have come here to study theatre. Thus when I am choosing plays, I am thinking about what would best serve the needs of my students in terms of giving them a range of quality production experiences and introducing them to the vast array of styles, genres, and playwrights that offer them the best possible training. Within those parameters, I then consider the needs and desires of the larger community. That consideration needs to extend beyond what kinds of productions might be most popular or appealing, though that is certainly a legitimate factor in choosing plays. I also try to pay attention to what is going on in the community or what I like to think of as "sniffing the air." What is the community thinking about? What kinds of conversations are happening in the dorms, classrooms, and dining halls? What current events are impacting the campus? Are there particular courses being offered, or an academic focus that could be supported by a particular play or production?

This is not to say that serving the community means every play has to have some type of serious, "relevant" topic. While theatre is an excellent way to explore issues and generate discussion, that is not the only way theatre can serve the community. Perhaps one of theatre's most important functions is to provide a venue for celebration and fun. Opportunities for people to relax and enjoy themselves as a group are vital to the life of a community, and shared laughter may be as life-affirming as a shared meal. Theatre also builds community through the sense of shared identity that comes from telling familiar stories or proclaiming common beliefs. We are drawn to the theatre to learn about the unknown and unfamiliar as well as to see ourselves and our own stories. Both functions are necessary for our communities to thrive.

My gut

Finally, I listen to my gut, to the "still small voice" within that I have learned to heed. While there are lots of plays on the list of projects I'd love to direct one day, at any given time there are always one or two that "hum." These are the plays that for whatever reason sparkle and dance in my imagination and that cause my brain to overflow with ideas for bringing the play to life through production. I've learned to honor this feeling for two important and related reasons. First, I believe that this is the way the Holy Spirit helps lead me to the "right" choice for any given production season. As I think about the needs of my students and my community, and as I consider different possibilities, I try to stay open and receptive to God's leading and

Engaging Culture—the Arts and Business

trust in "the hum." The second reason, which is really just an extension of the first, is that directing plays at Whitworth University is the path God has laid before me. If I believe that I am called to this job at this time, then I also must believe that God has given me the gifts, abilities, and desires to enable me to fulfill this call. My enthusiasm for and interest in various projects are not bonuses; they are an important aspect of the way God has equipped me for this work. So the final criteria for choosing a show is that it needs to be something I'm interested in directing; it has to be something that hums.

People who know me well—and particularly people who are familiar with the body of work I've directed over the years—might be surprised to hear me cite the Bible as one of my guides for choosing plays. After all, I have directed and taught plays that other Christian universities might tend to avoid. When I say biblical, I mean something quite different from what I generally encounter when others use this term. I most certainly do not mean the play subscribes to a specifically Christian point of view, promotes a particular moral or ethical stance, or has to be directly taken from Biblical sources. For many, the use of "biblical" as a defining term serves as a justification to limit both content and form, to set strict boundaries about what is appropriate or acceptable, and to screen out anything that might cause offense or discomfort and to keep us as Christian artists from going too far; however, I would argue that if we are truly using the Bible as our guide, then most Christian artists, myself included, don't go nearly far enough.

Andrea: Do you think the Bible is clear about what is right and what is wrong for performance issues?

Diana: Despite our faithful attendance at church, Bible study, and youth group, I fear we have in many ways lost sight of the true scope and power of the Bible and all it encompasses. Let me give an example from one of my classes. I was teaching a unit on contemporary performance art, one of the more cutting edge and controversial art practices in recent decades. I described various performative acts to my students, most of whom were shocked and outraged by the transgressive and confrontational nature of these performances. Some students even questioned my inclusion of these works in a course taught at a Christian university. What they did not know was that the examples I presented included three taken directly from the Old Testament: Ezekiel 12, where the prophet packs a bag and digs by hand through the wall of the city to symbolize Israel's coming exile; Jeremiah 19, where Jeremiah smashes a clay pot to demonstrate how God will smash Jerusalem unless they repent; and Ezekiel 12, which may be the most

81

elaborate example of performance art in the history of the world, where Ezekiel symbolizes the imminent siege of Jerusalem by building a model of the city, laying on his left side and eating a particular type of bread baked on cow dung for almost an entire year!

This little exercise in deception taught my students two very important things. First, they realized they did not know the Bible as well as they had thought. These were students at a Christian university, most of whom had grown up in Christian homes attending Sunday school and youth group, yet not one of them was familiar with these Old Testament stories. They recognized the names of the prophets and had some vague idea that the prophets had warned people of God's wrath, but they had no idea of the kinds of creative, provocative, and politically risky actions the prophets actually undertook. Second, these biblical accounts gave the students a fresh perspective on the controversial and political work of modern performance artists. Thinking about their own reactions to these contemporary works also gave them a new understanding of what the prophets had been up against and how the people of their time may have responded to them. When I reminded the students that God had commanded the prophets to enact these strange metaphoric performances that were as confrontational and potentially offensive in their time as some modern performances might seem to us, they were able to examine their own reactions in a new light and to look at difficult art through a lens of curiosity and grace.

Joy: How do you handle directing choices that you think are right but that the community is troubled by?

Diana: I know you've talked a little about the controversy surrounding decisions to produce the play *The Laramie Project*. Here are the Director's Notes from when we did *The Laramie Project*; these are my words to a largely Christian audience on presenting a "difficult" play:

> Several people have asked me why Whitworth Theatre has chosen to do *The Laramie Project* and there are a number of answers to that question. First, we try to give our theatre students a wide range of experiences as part of their theatre education, and this play's unique challenges as a documentary drama provide an exciting opportunity for them to master a different kind of theatrical style. Second, the play provides a forum for the Whitworth community to engage in the kind of courageous conversation we value as Christian scholars. Like other documentary plays, *The Laramie Project* refuses to provide easy answers or come to a specific conclusion about its topic. Instead, the play asks compelling questions

and presents multiple and often conflicting perspectives, inviting the audience to make sense of it all as best it can. In this way, the experience of seeing the play mirrors the experience of the people of Laramie as they tried to make sense of what occurred in their town. With post-play discussions, faculty panels, and prime-time dorm conversations, we seek to involve the campus in a dialogue about the issues raised by this play.

There is no question the content of *The Laramie Project* is challenging. The play stems from a horrific event: the beating death of a young man who could have been our student, friend, or son. The fact that this young man was gay, that his sexuality was a factor in his attack, and that the perpetrators were local boys makes the event even more difficult and troubling. But as we journey with the residents of Laramie, whose diverse views and responses mirror our own, we stand to gain new perspective about issues that raise difficult questions, trigger strong emotions and touch on our most deeply held beliefs. Finally, heartbreaking as it is, *The Laramie Project* is also a story of the tremendous compassion of which we are capable. And it is this testament to grace that is the play's ultimate gift to us. Thank you for being with us tonight.

Andrea: How do you deal with issues related to objectionable language?

Diana: Whitworth Theatre rarely produces plays on our main stage that contain profanity. Like many theatres, we tend to confine projects with controversial material or rough language to our smaller studio space and use the main auditorium for plays with a broader audience appeal. However, we chose to make an exception for *The Laramie Project* because we believed this play had the artistic, educational, and cultural value to merit a slot in our main stage season even though it contains material that might not be acceptable to all audiences.

People asked me why we didn't just edit the play and cut or substitute some of the language that could be considered offensive. The simple answer is that plays are copyrighted, and it is not legal to change the playwright's work without permission. There is, however, an even more significant issue. Even though characters in plays are fictional, they still represent real people in the sense that audiences recognize them and respond or relate to them in some way. Thus, as theatre artists we have an ethical responsibility to represent characters as authentically as possible. When we change what characters say or do to suit our own tastes, we are in a sense refusing to know or see them as the people they represent.

In the case of *The Laramie Project*, this moral imperative is even stronger because the characters in this play are in fact actual people from Laramie. The words in the script are transcriptions of their actual words. Our job as actors is to perform these people with the same respect and compassion we would give them were we to meet them in person. We may not like what they have to say or how they say it, but we have an obligation, as Father Roger Schmidt reminds us so eloquently in the play, to "say it right, say it correct."

Even in fictional plays, the same moral imperative applies. One of the first principles actors learn is that it is essential to love the character. One doesn't have to like the character, approve of them, or condone their behavior, but one absolutely must love the character unconditionally and without judgment if one is going to play them on stage. Characters are to be treated with the same respect we give to our fellow human beings. In this manner, acting is the most Christian of undertakings. After all, Jesus commands us to love one another, and not just that but to love as Jesus loves us: unconditionally and willing to lay down our very lives for one another. So it is with the actor. We must be willing to "lay down our lives," including our judgments and assumptions, and present the character with honesty and dignity to the best of our abilities. To refuse to play a character as written is to refuse to accept the people that character represents. Moreover, to change a character's language is turn their story into a lie.

A few years ago, Whitworth did a production of Arthur Miller's *All My Sons*. This classic example of American Realism set in the years following World War II tells the story of Joe Keller, a much-admired family man and pillar of the community, who is hiding the fact that he shipped out defective airplane parts resulting in the deaths of several young pilots and then let his partner take the fall. The play is a powerful fable about corporate greed, personal cowardice, and moral responsibility. The production was highly successful, but I received a complaint from a woman who had brought her teenage granddaughter to the play and was offended that the character used the words "goddamn it" and "hell." This patron did not think a Christian university should present characters that used such language, but that is who Joe Keller *is*. He represents a particular kind of man with a certain set of values and traits, and those things are embodied in the way he speaks and the words he chooses as surely as they are in his actions. This is as true of Joe Keller's rough language as it is of Hamlet's beautiful soliloquies. We can no more change the way Joe Keller talks then we can change the fact that he knowingly sent those defective parts. Happily, I was able to share that perspective with the patron who in turn had a thought-provoking conversation with her daughter about the play and the characters.

Tom: Thank you so much, Diana. Now, let me introduce Ben Brody. Ben did his graduate work at the University of Washington. He writes hymns and directs worship and music at churches in addition to his teaching. Ben, I know you've thought a lot about the virtue of humility as it relates to the discipline of music. What sorts of things do you think we should be keeping in mind?

Ben: One of my favorite quotes is from Norvin Richards. He said, "Humility consists . . . in understanding oneself so well that one is disinclined to over-estimation."

Humility can be defined as having a true understanding of one's own abilities and gifts. In Matthew's gospel, Jesus offers himself as an example of humility when he says "Take my yoke upon you and learn from me; for I am gentle and humble in heart, and you will find rest for your souls" (Matt 11:29). In the *Magnificat*, Mary describes how God "lifts up the humble in heart", but also how God responds to one of humility's corresponding vices as God has "scattered the proud in the thoughts of their hearts" (Luke 1:46–55).

If humility is a right estimation of one's own abilities, it is centered between the two vices of excess and deficiency: overestimation of one's abilities (pride) and underestimation of one's abilities (false modesty). Pride is a vice that is often easily recognizable. It is a vice that has had an intoxicating effect on musicians from Jean-Baptiste Lully to Richard Wagner to John Lennon ("more popular than Jesus"). Pride exhibits itself in music as having a higher view in one's abilities than one deserves. A prideful musician will find it difficult to accept a loss as being just and will frequently look to blame the setback on other factors (unfair judging, problems with the instrument, etc.).

False modesty, or underestimating one's abilities, is perhaps the less recognized but equally damaging vice and one that seems particularly problematic in some Christian circles. We Christians are usually good at recognizing pride, but often less astute at recognizing or at least correcting false modesty. This likely comes out of our vigilance to correct pride, yet false humility can be just as damaging as pride, particularly in the discipline of music. For musicians to excel, they have to have a vision for what they can accomplish if they are diligent in their pursuit of excellence. False modesty is a refusal to acknowledge one's true ability, which hinders the musician's ability to progress and excel.

For musicians, humility takes different forms in the various contexts in which we do our work. A musician may spend hours alone preparing for a single performance of a five minute piece. There is a public side of our work, but it is relatively small compared to the "private" time spent rehearsing. What does humility look like in the practice room? Perhaps it means considering multiple options for interpreting a passage of music, rather than just settling on the one that first comes to mind. Simply submitting to the discipline of practice is a humble acknowledgement that our gifts require discipline and repetition.

In the lesson, we teachers have a profound influence on our students which can easily be abused. Do we pay attention to the balance between imitation and independence in lessons? Do we model good technique but also encourage students to look to other models as well through recordings and masterclasses, recognizing that there is not one "perfect" interpretation? What does humility look like in a large ensemble rehearsal? Or in performance?

The antidote to both pride and false modesty is the recovery of a true understanding of humility. As teachers, there is much that we can do to aid our students in this recovery. Here are a few practical suggestions.

Lift up examples of true humility in lessons and ensemble rehearsals. J.S. Bach is one example of a musician who seemed to exemplify both a lack of pride and a lack of false modesty. Look for examples among students as well as in popular culture and encourage students to identify and reflect on examples themselves.

Develop a discerning eye for false modesty, and address it when necessary. False modesty seems to be a problem to which some female students are particularly prone, perhaps because they are not encouraged to pursue leadership roles. Give students honest assessments of their abilities, and give them opportunities for self-assessment. Ask critical questions if their self-assessments seem too high or too low.

Encourage students to take risks and accept that failure (losing a competition or missing a note) is an important part of the life of any musician. Teach students that strong leadership and initiative is not incompatible with humility.

Help students recognize that there is nothing inherently arrogant or prideful about performance, but that our humility or lack thereof is exhibited in how we respond to criticism or praise. Model positive ways to respond to both praise and criticism and insist on students modeling this for each other. Create opportunities for students to perform and give feedback to each other.

Tom: Thank you Ben, that gives us a lot to think about. Our next speaker is Craig Hinnenkamp. He did his graduate work at Gonzaga University but before that gained over twenty five years of management related experience with companies and government agencies including Washington State Labor and Industries. His focus is on faith in the field of business. He is going to talk to us about the tension between consistency and rigidity in the workplace.

Craig: One of the most frequent comparisons between the practice of leadership and management is that of art versus science. As a science, management practice seeks to control variability, eliminate personal preference, and focus on the consistent application of policy in practice. Leadership, on the other hand, recognizes the often extreme variability in real life situations and the difficulty in consistent enforcement of policy particularly in the realm of personnel policy.

My own personal experience in this area spans approximately thirty years of management/leadership practice. I have found that although consistency in the application of policy is important, it is a short hop to rigidity in policy application if one disallows the consideration of the variability in specific situations. It is most important that the leader/manager approach decision-making from a consistent set of moral principles rather than only strict adherence to the specific letter of policy.

To clarify this, consider the following story based upon a true situation I dealt with as a young manager approximately thirty years ago. As a young manager in a large timber based corporation, one of my assignments was to create and establish an Employee Assistance Program in the company's largest facility. Employee assistance programs were relatively new to industry at this time and traditionally trained older managers struggled with the concept and were very skeptical regarding this type of programs, their contribution to profitability, and other measures of organizational success. Many felt it set a dangerous precedent in terms of personnel management practices.

The philosophies associated with employee assistance programs, and later extension into employee wellness programs, argued for a more holistic approach to management of the human resource. They acknowledged that the hiring of an employee involved the whole person, and could not, in reality, exclude the employee's personal, as well as family, issues (chronic illness in the family, substance abuse, emotional health, etc.). Well-managed employee assistance programs allowed employers to provide access to professional services such as mental health counseling, alcohol, and substance abuse treatment presented the opportunity for employers to keep valued employee resources and at the same time continue to hold people accountable to employment performance standards.

John Brown was a senior employee in this timber-based corporation having started at the age of eighteen and worked in a variety of positions over a twenty-five year period. John, at the time of this incident, worked in the paper mill in a lead position in the rolling mill. John was a well-known and respected individual in the community, an elder in a local Christian church, and volunteer in numerous community activities. For twenty-five years, in fact, John was a model employee in the company, a hard worker with an exceptional work ethic, and a mentor to younger employees as they started and moved up through the organization.

Over a three-month period, however, a change occurred. A marked change in John's attitude at work, his relationships with other employees and his overall performance was documented in accordance with a disciplinary policy. John's behavior ultimately resulted in his termination at the end of this three-month period. Most notable among John's changing behaviors was a substantive increase in unexcused absences from work. John used up all available sick leave as well as vacation leave, and still absenteeism increased. This absenteeism worsened over time as John would often leave work with no notification to his superiors, placing the responsibility to pick up his work load on his peers.

We were perplexed and confused about the substantive change in John's behaviors during this period; John appeared to be unreceptive to offers for employee assistance if needed, a central facet of the employee assistance program in disciplinary cases, and the responsible manager felt he had no choice according to disciplinary policy but to move in this progressive manner. With great sadness the manager recommended John's termination from the company for excessive absenteeism over a three-month period.

Jane Smith was the plant nurse and also a long term employee of the company who was well known and trusted by all who worked in the facility. As one of my direct reports, Jane came to me after John had been terminated and suggested there was something very wrong in this situation

Engaging Culture—the Arts and Business

and that we had erred in terminating John. She felt there was something significant going on behind the scenes in the family that John could not, or at least felt he could not, discuss, and she argued that she could get to the bottom of this if she was allowed to pursue the matter privately. I agreed that it seemed appropriate to find out what we could in this situation. If nothing else it would help us learn what we could do better in the area of employee assistance.

In relatively short order, Jane found that John's fourteen-year-old daughter had run away from home and was attempting to live on the streets in a nearby metropolitan area. She had apparently been experimenting with drugs, and neither John nor his wife was equipped to deal with this kind of a problem with their own child. The matter worsened when John found that his daughter had also become involved in prostitution, and he had no idea how to find her and get her back home. Because of his position as elder in the church and his status in the community, John felt that he had to keep this matter secret and felt there was no place of safety in which he might be able to share the difficulties involved in the situation and seek some help.

I felt very strongly that we had erred in our decision to terminate not because we hadn't followed established disciplinary policy but because we had. When I presented the information to the Director of Personnel, his initial response was the same as before. We had offered access to employee assistance and John chose not to avail himself of that help. As such the matter was really none of our concern at that point. My argument remained that the purpose of employee assistance and the management philosophy associated with it was to recognize the difficulties all of us encounter in life, and to provide a mechanism by which we can assist our employees during these difficulties. Moreover, this would allow us to keep a valuable resource.

Jane and I decided to essentially conduct an intervention with John, present to him what we knew to be true, and to seek the possibility to offer assistance. Although not in a position to guarantee anything to John, I argued that if he would allow us to work with him confidentially, we might be able to help him recover his daughter and reestablish his employment with the company. He agreed to cooperate, and when I argued with the Director of Personnel to reconsider the termination in lieu of John's willingness to participate with employee assistance, he also agreed.

Having the agreement of both parties, we proceeded to involve John with local authorities who were able to find John's daughter and return her to her home in relatively short order. John was assisted in locating confidential family counseling services for his daughter and the rest of the family. John was reappointed to his former position in a probationary status pending satisfactory performance over a six-month period, which he successfully completed and was then restored to full duty.

To summarize, from a strict management perspective, the decision to terminate after a progressive disciplinary process was technically correct. But, from an integrated leadership perspective, it was not the "right" moral decision. The net outcome was the salvation and restoration of a valuable employee resource to the company but also a much more loyal and appreciative employee who recognized the espoused values of the company were also evident in action.

Tom: Thank you to all of our guests. It's wonderful to be able to talk with others who share our commitment to shaping the next generation of Christian citizens.

Discussion Questions

1. Does your school have conflicts related to the arts? How are these resolved?
2. Do you see a gender difference when you think about how students experience humility or confidence?
3. What Christian business people might be invited into your school to help students think about their future work? What about workers in other fields?

10

Athletics in a Christian High School

PRINCIPAL TOM ANDERSON OPENED *the Parent-Teacher-Student Association meeting with prayer and then introduced the topic for the evening.*

"We've been having a lot of discussion here on the role athletics does and should play in our school. Most of us have strong opinions on the topic, and so we agreed that we need to have someone who has thought seriously about our questions come and meet with us this evening. Professor Kevin Vande Streek is the Director of the Spoelhof Fieldhouse Complex at Calvin College and is also the men's basketball coach. Many of you know him because your kids have one or both of his books Strong and Courageous – Joshua's Lesson for Athletes (And the Cheering Section) and Lasting Victory: Meditations for Students, Athletes, Coaches and Those Who Cheer Them On.[41]

"We are delighted to have Kevin with us. Before we begin with our questions, Coach, will you start off by telling us why you think athletics is so important?"

Kevin: Any time I think through a bigger topic I like to start with three basic questions of Reformed thinking: Who am I? Why am I here? Where am I going? Briefly, I am a child of God. I have been created by Him and have a purpose in this life to serve and praise Him. The Bible teaches that because I believe in God I will go to Heaven for eternity. I have in no way earned this gift and am a fallen sinner; but by the Grace of God, he has chosen me and washed away my sin. Because of His love for me, I want to live a life that honors and glorifies Him.

---

41. Kevin Vande Streek's two books can be ordered from: Calvin College Campus Store, 1745 Knollcrest Circle SE, Grand Rapids, MI 49546. Telephone: 1-800-748-0122.

Sport is certainly contained under this umbrella. I think there are several reasons why we have sport, but let me touch on three. First, we can celebrate a joyous life in Christ. Playing sports is fun and is the primary reason we should play. God created us spiritually, physically, emotionally, and socially; and He created play as a way for us to express our love and joy. Because of Christ's life, death, and resurrection, we can celebrate this life. Play is a great opportunity to honor God.

Second, we have athletics to help us live a healthy and balanced life. The world is a sinful place with workaholics, materialism, poor diet and exercise. We always seem to strive for the next thing and not enjoy the moment. Sport is so big in our culture, and sin has so distorted it that as Reformed thinkers we can take responsibility to try educating and bringing play back to its original goodness. A break from our workday and the stress of life for physical activity, fitness, training, and nutrition is a part of a healthy life. A routine of sport, play, recreation, nutrition and rest isn't necessarily about living longer; it's about living happy and healthy, and being a more productive servant in the Kingdom.

Third, we have athletics for the education gained and lessons learned. Our classrooms are fabulous, but in the field we can take what we are being taught and demonstrate what we have learned. In the field we find out what are weaknesses are. We can push others and ourselves to see our character and values be challenged and grow. We are a fallen people, so sin affects our play as well as every other aspect of life; but we can ask Christ for forgiveness and move forward. The list of lessons we can learn in athletics seems endless including humility, social interaction, relationship building, goal setting, self-sacrifice, determination, trust, accountability, competition, character, integrity, leadership, followership, responsibility, roles, confidence, values, communication, team work, and winning and losing with grace.

Tom: I suppose Athletics fits in with the Creation-Fall-Redemption motif as well?

Kevin: Absolutely. God created the world and everything in it including play. The fall affects all areas of life including sport. The world is full of examples of this from off the field extra-marital affairs to using steroids or blood doping to gain an illegal advantage. There are coaches who have illegally recruited athletes and boosters who have made payments to players. We as Christians have a responsibility to try to bring all aspects of life back toward their original goodness. We can do this through teaching, coaching, encouraging, and mentoring our young people to play with joy, emotion, and passion and to play competitively but responsibly. I can think of nowhere else where would I want my children to play sports than in a Christian environment.

Parent: C.S. Lewis said that sports don't so much build character as reveal it. Do you think that is true?

Kevin: Far be it from me to contradict C.S. Lewis, but I believe sport does both. I would certainly say that sport reveals character. I've seen phenomenal examples of positive character shown in the athletic arena: tennis players who've called balls in or golfers who've called a penalty on themselves even though it was to their own detriment. I've seen a softball player who after batting and hurting her knee be carried around the bases by two opponents who helped her score a run. I've seen opponents help each other off the floor, pat each other on the back, and even hug after grueling contests. Remember that the entire world has fallen into sin, and so I've heard foul language used and seen poor treatment of players, coaches, and officials. I've seen lying, cheating, and terrible incidents of fans fighting or burning cars in the street following games. Be prepared for mistakes. In a Christian environment, we choose to hold people accountable for poor decisions and actions with truth and grace. We encourage positive behavior, and we challenge a change in poor behavior for the purpose of honoring God. This is how character can be built.

Student: I heard that if Tiger Woods accidentally moved his golf ball without being seen, he would call a penalty on himself because he is so honest about the game; yet in his personal life, he lied and cheated on his wife and family. Does honesty in sports influence one's honesty in life?

Kevin: My simple answer to this one is I hope so. In our basketball program at Calvin, we have devotions before every game. I explain to our guys that we don't do these devotions so God will help us win a game, although He does this; it is so that we understand that our faith and our living for Him should be done in all areas of life, including something seemingly as insignificant as a basketball game. We pray for wisdom, patience, intensity, for our opponents, our safety, and that we can bring honor to God through our play. Abraham Kuyper's idea that every square inch belongs to God certainly includes athletics. I would hope that through the prayers prayed, the lessons learned, and character being built in athletics that we would also educate people that these lessons would apply to all aspects of our lives-faith, community, relationships, profession, etc.

Bonnie: What advice would you give our coaches?

Kevin: I would start with the idea that the mission of Christian education is to help train young people to go out and serve in Christ's kingdom. With that in mind, I ask myself as a coach what my role is in that. This is a huge responsibility, and I know I can't do it alone; but I also know my players can't grow into who God wants them to become without me. Work to develop your own faith, live your life, and treat the people you come in contact with as a model for those you are coaching. Be someone who models Christ with a balance of both truth and grace. Challenge your players to grow in their faith. Make sure they are having fun. Challenge them to work really hard, to work together, to improve their character, and to get better at their skill. Be demanding and have high expectations. A high school coach should play to win the game. Winning isn't everything, but striving to win is at the very heart of competitive sport and is very important in so many ways. A choir director pushes members to give their best performance possible, as do teachers, and coaches should be no different; but remember, the reasons for participating surpass the outcome of the contest.

Parent: Do athletic practices and games take precedence over everything else—family, church activities, and so forth? Are we sending the wrong message to our young people that nothing matters but the responsibility to their athletic team?

Kevin: As a former player and now coach, commitment to a team and teammates is very important, but these aren't more important than quality family time. When compared to church activities, it's a bit more of a quagmire as we need to realize that we are not comparing the importance of faith to participating in a sport. We're comparing sport practices and games to young people's group activities. A fact to consider is that there are now more opportunities than ever before. Not only are there sports, but there are a multitude of sports to choose from, and a variety of travel teams from AAU to Junior Olympic Volleyball. Along with multiple sport opportunities are dance, children's choir, theater, mission projects, etc.

Scheduling all activities requires cooperation between family, sport, and church activities, and some choosing must take place. Choices need to be made, and balance and moderation is a great guideline. We certainly do not want activities to overshadow faith and family. My suggestion is for parents and students to get information on schedules in advance and talk through pros, cons, and possible conflicts. Communication with coaches and directors is probably necessary, and then decisions can be made as to what to participate in. I'm big on commitment, so if someone decides to participate they need to commit to the expectations of the program.

My advice in choosing activities starts when children are young. Encourage them to start in a variety of opportunities with a lower level of commitment. As they grow older and narrow choices, a more advanced level of play and commitment becomes more of a possibility. In high school, this should probably get narrowed down to two or three things to be involved in. Families and family life do not have to revolve around sport. There are programs and levels of play that don't include needing to travel every weekend.

Parents need to set the precedent but need to make these decisions before committing to participate. I would agree that families in general miss too much time around the dinner table and Sunday worship. I would encourage people to think about why their children are playing and who they are playing for. When you look at an issue and start with thinking about the big picture and your philosophy, it helps make smaller decisions and commitments to priorities easier.

Parent: Besides helping with selection of activities, what is the parent's role in athletics for their children?

Kevin: Parents today are very involved in their children's sport participation. Driving, meals, laundry, and finances are all crucial in order for involvement. Encouragement and support of their child, their teammates, and their coaches is invaluable. Parents need to keep the big picture of why to participate in sports in perspective and help teach it to their children.

I grew up in a house where the coach was always right, the teacher was always right, and the pastor was always right. Even though they might not always have been, this philosophy taught me invaluable lessons. Often times I didn't get my way, and I had to deal with sitting on the bench, being yelled at by my coach, having to stay after school, or having to memorize extra Bible passages. I learned discipline, patience, and perseverance through both set-backs and successes. My parents taught me that who I am is bigger than my performance on the athletic field or in the classroom, and my parents were bigger than my performance as well.

So often today we want our children to be successful and to have no road blocks that our complaints to teachers and coaches, often done with our children's knowledge, hurt our children greatly. Our children are not infallible. They can do things wrong, and sometimes they are simply not as good or as talented as other children in a particular area. This is a reality in life. There's a saying that 10 percent of life is about what happens to us and 90 percent is how we react to it. I think we can do a much better job teaching our children how to work through the 90 percent than what we are currently doing.

When our children hurt, and we hurt with them, I would advise parents to resist the urge to call, email, or text negative feelings of blame to someone else and help work through the situation in a Christian manner with our child. Valuable lessons can be learned when our children don't get the role they'd like. If our high school students have a question about playing time, encourage them to set up an appointment with the coach and ask. They can write their questions in a letter format if it would be easier. Certainly this teaches responsibility and standing up for themselves. Teachers and coaches are not perfect, but schools have hired the best candidates possible. It is their job to make decisions and educate to the best of their abilities. A parent's job is to educate and encourage their children.

Tom: We've covered why and how players should play and the role of coaches and parents. If you came to a basketball game against our big rival, what would you hope to see from our spectators?

Kevin: I would hope the crowd would be loud and boisterous! At the same time I hope they would be respectful of opponents and officials and stand quietly and respectfully during the national anthem. Our opponents, even rivals, make the game possible. Games do not have to be a bitter struggle between combatants. Our opponents help us achieve our best. Even if they are playing in a way we don't like, they challenge us to show our Christ-like demeanor. I have known and currently know many officials. Like all of us coaches and players, some are more talented than others. But I can say the officials I know are outstanding men and women who love the athletes and love the game. They work to provide a service, and they take their craft very seriously. We owe them a great deal of respect and thanks. Like I tell our players, 'You can't go to church on Sunday and call our faith good for the week. God calls us to be faithful in everything we do at all times. We can't go to a sporting event as a spectator and check our faith at the door. We are sinful and make mistakes, but the big picture of Christ-like behavior is our goal.' Again, spectators should be positive and supportive.

Joy: Should football be a part of a Christian education athletic program?

Kevin: I don't have a problem with football being a part of a Christian education athletic program. I know the concern is that football is an aggressive game and injuries are a reality. Concussions especially are in the news regularly. On the other hand, the Bible calls us to be lambs of God and to love our neighbor. I've heard people ask how football players can be lambs and yet hit someone with as much force as they can muster. A football player or coach might counter with this text from James 1: 2–4, *"Consider it pure joy, my brothers, whenever you face trials of many kinds, because you know that the testing of your faith develops."* The coach would explain that football presents a great test, because after a player gets knocked down they need to get control of their emotions, get back up, and make another play. Like other sports, football provides great opportunity for team work, discipline, and communication among other things to be developed. There is a high chance of injury when playing football, and studies would prove this; however, injuries are at a high risk in soccer, lacrosse, and other sports as well. One NCAA study shows that football is third on the list of producing the most concussions behind men's ice hockey and women's soccer. With new medical information preventing and treating concussions and improved equipment, football is a legitimate option for young athletes.

Bonnie: What is our responsibility as a school to help players in their college selection process if they are being recruited by college coaches?

Kevin: In all honesty, I'm not sure the school has any more responsibility to help student athletes in their college selection process than with students who are not athletes. Guidance counselors can help students understand what their academic strengths are, provide information on colleges, help with social and emotional fit, write recommendations, and send academic test scores and transcripts. Coaches can provide some help with sending out game tapes when asked, provide a reference of the character and work ethic of the player, and maybe help a player sort through recruiting letters, calls, and texts. The majority of the process falls to the parents and the student.

My suggestion is to start the college search process with two questions: What talents and gifts has God given me? And who does God want me to become? Notice I didn't say 'what.' I said 'who.' Move on from there with lots of prayer throughout the process. Developing as a whole person regardless of whether you are talented athletically enough to be a professional athlete or not would be the important thing to discover. I would suggest visiting five schools beginning as early as the spring of the junior year and meet as many people as you can while visiting. This would include professors, coaches, and players. Apply to at least three schools early in the fall of the senior year, complete financial aid forms in January, and apply for as many scholarships as possible. Maybe visit and stay overnight a second time with the two top choices in the spring.

What academic gifts and interests a student has should help narrow things down. For example, someone who has a 30 ACT and wants a great business school will direct that person's college search. Athletic opportunities are another area to search. In today's world, there really aren't athletic secrets. If you have the ability to play Division I sports, those coaches will know about you and offer you a scholarship if they want you. Finances are also a big concern just like they are for Christian day school and high school and need to be considered, but it can't be the only issue. Study hard now and make getting good grades a high priority. Academic scholarships are a great way to offset college costs. Lastly, college is not the military. If you invest in your first year and it's not the fit you wanted, you can transfer. You're not locked in for four years. When you get to college, get involved. If not in sports, then get involved in other organizations, floor activities, chapels, and intramurals.

High School Coach: How much should we as coaches and athletes speak about our faith when we are interviewed by the media?

Kevin: Our basketball players at Calvin can readily talk about the NBA. They can talk about what team is winning, what player had a good scoring night the night before, and argue non-stop about who is the best between any two given players; yet we as Christians are uncomfortable talking about our faith sometimes. I tell our guys the reason they can talk so well on the NBA is that they read about it, watch it, watch SportsCenter highlights on ESPN, and discuss the game constantly. Because of all that time, thought, and energy, the NBA is a big part of who they are.

We need to read more of the Bible, pray, listen to Christian music, and discuss what we've read, seen, or heard. If we do, our faith will continue to grow in us, and we'll talk about it more freely. Our men's basketball program at Calvin actually has a two-page guideline document for talking to the media. I want people to be natural and not fake but also to be able to get their point across. Knowing that God is the giver of their talent and God's grace is what allows us to be successful, I would think and hope that this would come out in conversation. If the opportunity or moment is right, we should thank God in the interview. Tim Tebow of the New York Jets is a fabulous role model when talking to the media, but even he doesn't mention his faith in every interview. I think it's a great idea for coaches to encourage their athletes to talk about their faith when they can and compliment a player when she or he does so.

Parent: NCAA president Miles Brand said that schools should be held accountable for poor academic performance on the part of players. Is youth sport too aggressive in our culture?

Kevin: We have a hard time balancing the culture of youth sport in our society and even in our own families. I don't like the idea that everyone gets a trophy for just participating. I think it encourages complacency. My wife and I don't agree on youth soccer ties; she loves them and thinks everyone goes home happy because they didn't lose. I don't like ties and think everyone goes home unhappy because no one won. Striving to win is important, but sport in general and the pursuit of victory is not the most important thing. We've all seen or heard the overbearing parent who screams at the ref or coach about a call or playing time. We've also seen the overbearing coach who screams and yells at the players as if the world championship is on the line. Both of these are extreme examples of too aggressive of a sport culture.

Are we not hopeful that our children will strive to win in life, to overcome adversity, to learn perseverance, and learn mental and physical toughness? Unfortunately our children will grow up and face accidents, disease, poverty, and the utmost challenge of defeating the evil one. The great thing is that we know Christ has already won and that everything is a part of his plan. So in that sense, the outcome of the sporting contest is already been determined. Play hard. Play together. Have fun. Strive. Persevere. Compete. Enjoy spectating. Work through and around roadblocks. Be thankful to the Giver for the talents and abilities and opportunities to play.

Student: How does athletics help develop leadership?

Kevin: Before we can lead others, we need to be able to lead ourselves. This is probably our most difficult task. We need to work very hard to build our relationship with Christ our Savior. Athletics allow us to put into practice what we know and what we are being taught about leadership.

When it comes to leading others I think trust is the foundation of any successful relationship. I am thinking of trust that is built through shared experiences over time. Once trust is built there can be effective communication. This means more than discussing the cute boy who is in the back of the room or how sweet your new football cleats are. Effective communication requires really getting to know others on your team. This can include being vulnerable and asking tough questions of yourself and others.

When a team can communicate, they can come to consensus on what they are committed to. I'm a big believer in goal setting, but not in setting outcome-based goals. So many things come into play with winning games or a championship and that are out of the players' and coach's control. I prefer process goals because they can be controlled. Commitment to off-season work-outs, weight training, team chemistry, and off the field behavior are great process goals.

When goals have been set, accountability is necessary. Although the world tells us other people are not our business, this is not what the Bible says. We should be concerned with others and do our best to help each other walk on the narrow path. I'd use a Jiffy Lube oil change place as an example. When you are about to drive your car into the garage, there is a person who directs you so that you don't drive your car in the hole. That's accountability. We should not be afraid to hold others accountable, and we should be thankful when someone cares enough to hold us accountable. Leaders are people who will help ensure that trust, communication, commitment, and accountability are a part of a team culture. Athletics provide great opportunity for this to be developed, and the best team results occur when this type of culture is accomplished. These lessons in leadership can be applied to any area of life.

Student: Who were your mentors?

Kevin: My personal mentors would first be my parents. I grew up in a Christian home and always felt loved and encouraged. We never missed church, had devotions at the supper table, and my parents sacrificed to send my sister and me to Christian schools. I spent a lot of time with my grandfather doing carpentry work and going fishing. I still reflect on his calm, caring, and Christ-like demeanor.

Second, the coaches I had in high school were my biggest mentors in the sport arena. My varsity basketball coach, Bart Bruins, was very intense. He demanded our greatest effort and our best performance. Most games we played we had less talent than our opponents had; but because of our effort and team play, we were able to come out with a victory. Mr. Bruins had the highest integrity, loved sport, and loved to compete. That made a big impact on me. My high school biology teacher Dennis De Kok was also my cross country, junior varsity basketball, and track coach. He is the biggest reason I wanted to teach and coach. He also was demanding and a great teacher in the classroom, in the athletic realm, and in life. These men loved God, loved their families, and loved their students. Even though these two men challenged me, and at times I didn't like it, I knew they cared very much for me and my team mates and wanted us to grow and develop.

Parent: What impact did your faith have on your play?

Kevin: I think my faith impacted my play without me thinking much about it. We were always taught to be respectful, appreciative, and grateful. My coaches made sure we behaved on the floor, showed respect for officials and opponents, and made sure we knew that God is who made our play possible. As a youngster, I don't think I thought much about my faith in sport; so I am very thankful that my coaches and mentors did, and that they guided me in the right direction.

Dave: What are your thoughts about team selection, cutting people who try out, and playing time?

Kevin: I would say I'm opposed to cutting before high school. I understand that in some situations there aren't enough uniforms or facilities or coaches, and so there probably need to be cuts. Athletic success before high school does not necessarily predict success in high school, and I think the opportunity to play on a team and be coached is valuable for anyone who is interested in playing. Now if a player doesn't show up for practice regularly or horses around when they are there, that's a different story. I just think there are so many valuable things to learn through participating that as many as possible should get a chance to be on the team.

When talking about high school sports, the emphasis now is on developing those who are most gifted in this area. The lower the coach-to-player ratio the better and more personal the instruction is that can take place. For example, one year I coached a junior varsity basketball team that combined freshmen and sophomores. Most teams would normally keep twelve players, but this particular year I decided to keep seventeen. It was great in that five more players got to be a part of the team, but I felt bad that the better players did not get as much attention from me as they probably deserved. I didn't do that again.

As for playing time, not everyone plays first chair trumpet or gets a part in the school play. Not everyone is gifted enough to get playing time on a given team. I also don't feel the year a player is in school should be a limitation. If a sophomore is the most talented keeper on the soccer team, she should be the starter. I think that a big goal for the high school coach is to win the game, and normally that would mean that not everyone would get to play.

Andrea: What about excellence? Isn't a Christian called to be excellent?

Kevin: My first response to that is that God calls us to be faithful, not successful. We certainly want to strive to be our best in everything we do, so to what extent do we pursue excellence? Athletes who quit everything else and work solely on their sport would probably get much better at it than just practicing a couple of hours a day. There still needs to be a balance to life. John Wooden, former legendary UCLA men's basketball coach, is famous for saying to do your best and when you have you should feel satisfied. One of my life's greatest experiences was to be able to spend a day with Coach Wooden. Being the Calvinist I am, I asked him, "How do you know when you've done your best? It always seems to me there is more that can be done." He just talked about living a balanced life, making a plan, and doing your very best within that plan. I guess that's how I'd define excellence.

Tom: Coach Vande Streek, thank you so much for being here today. Is there anything you'd like to add in summary?

Kevin: Let me sum up by saying that I'm not standing up on a pedestal and speaking down to the masses. In fact, I often say I stand in the front of the "mess up" line. I have made more than my share of mistakes and poor decisions in my nearing fifty years of playing and coaching. I am thankful to God for His Throne of Grace where I can lay down these errors and then press on to improve. I continue to strive to be a Christian in the world of sport. What I would suggest to everyone is to spend time thinking and praying about the role of sport in our lives. Our culture has overvalued, over emphasized, and, in general, made a sinful mess of sport. We, as Christians, are called to be in the world but not of it. If done correctly, sport can be beautiful act of worship. Let's all do our very best to strive toward this goal.

Discussion Questions

1. What role do athletics play in your high school?
2. Have there been times when your community has talked about some of the issues raised here?

11

Life after High School

DAVID: SO IT'S MY turn to take the podium. Most of you already know that I joined the military shortly after graduating from this school. What you might not know is that I did so because I had absolutely no clue as to what to do with the next part of my life. I wasn't that great of a student while I was here because I had no personal goals and no sense of direction for the future. I would not blame the school nor would I blame my parents for that fact. It is just how it was.

A survey of students in grades seven and eight in seventeen Christian schools throughout the United States and Canada asked the question: *In what area do you think you might like to work when you are an adult? Some areas might be agriculture and farming, science, building as an architect or carpenter, medical as a doctor or nurse, math, television, journalism as reporter or writer, teacher, and many other areas. Why would you like to work in that area? If you never think about the work you might do as an adult, please say so.*[42]

Girls responded to the question by describing their plans to work in a great many different fields, both professional and technical; however, boys tended to have unrealistic dreams such as playing basketball or football at the professional level. If they would be unable to do that they would then go to work with their fathers. There is nothing wrong with boys wanting to follow in their father's footsteps. What is wrong is that they seem to allow themselves few other options or goals to consider. That's where I was.

---

42. Stronks and Stronks, *Families Living in the Fabric of Faithfulness: Parents and Children Describe What Works.*

I've read that if by grade six kids have some sense of direction for their future they will go through high school and further education more successfully. It doesn't take a rocket scientist to figure that out.

You asked our committee to explore whether we can do a better job of helping students who enter our high school explore what the future might hold for them. We've come up with a plan that we are presenting to you as a draft or as a beginning of discussion. Our goal for this plan is to help our students think about their own thinking ability, about their own interests, and about God's calling for their lives. That is a tall order, but we hope you agree it's a worthy goal.

In helping students learn to think about their own thinking, we suggest that every ninth grade student take the Myers-Briggs Type Indicator. Students can take this test in class in a forty-five minute period. Bonnie will score each MBTI and then have a meeting with groups of students to share the data and what it means to them. The outcome will show students how they 'recharge their batteries.'

I realize that most of you know the Myers-Briggs really well, but here is a quick summary. If you want to read more about it you can find it at http://www.myersbriggs.org

- *Introverts can be very sociable but need quiet to reflect, concentrate, and understand the world.*
- *Extraverts prefer learning through interaction with others and are more action-oriented.*
- *Sensing people are detail-oriented, want facts, and trust them.*
- *Intuitive people seek out patterns and relationships among the facts and look for the big picture.*
- *Thinking people value fairness, focus on logic, and look for objective criteria in making a decision.*
- *Feeling people focus more on human values and needs as they make decisions.*
- *Judging people are decisive and focus on completing the task, taking actions quickly.*
- *Perceptive people are curious and spontaneous, start many tasks, and often find it difficult to meet a deadline.*

Life after High School

We believe students will enjoy learning about themselves and that this information will partially explain to them why they react to situations the way they do. We also want them to see that there are several legitimate weaknesses and strengths in each set of indicators.

In order to help our students understand the options that are open to them, once every week during the ninth grade year we plan to have someone from our community come to tell students about his or her work, what the future looks like in that kind of work, what the work is like on a day-to-day basis, how one prepares for that kind of work, and the joys and problems they encounter. We are certain we can identify people who would be willing to share their journey and also talk about how they, as Christians, live out that work. We will want to offer to help with any charts or other visuals that would help to explain their field. This is our first step in helping our students understand some of the options available to them.

During their tenth grade year, each student will select one of the options they have learned about. They will research that area and write a paper describing the work that is involved, the educational process or internship that would prepare one for that kind of work, challenges a Christian would find in that field, and describe why their particular gifts might be used in that line of work. This paper will be written in students' English classes using appropriate writing techniques; however, the students will have access to all of their teachers and may discuss the paper with them.

During year eleven, each student will have an on-site interview with someone who works in an area that interests them. In their social studies class, prior to the interview, the students will talk about questions that are suitable to ask. They will record the interview and submit the transcript of the interview to the teacher.

Year twelve students will, in teams of three, talk to the ninth grade classes about their reactions to the experiences they had while working through this project in grades nine, ten, and eleven. They will describe their own plans for the future, their uncertainties and ways they hope to work through them, what their next step will be concerning tertiary education, and whether or not the whole project helped them.

You can see that we are trying to construct a culture of learning in which students learn to think about themselves and their own futures in God's Kingdom. This is really just an outline that will need lots of tinkering and adjustment as we work through it. So our committee is eager to hear your reactions and comments.

Joe: I'm going to come right out and say what lots of us are thinking. We already are struggling to cover the content we need to cover in our classes. What you are describing will take away from teaching time. Is it really worth doing that?

Dave: I guess it all depends on what we, as teachers, see is the task of a Christian high school. If our job is covering content then we won't have time for everything. If helping kids think about their future lives is "icing on the cake," then it is not worth doing. Our committee believes that if we truly are trying to build a culture in which students reflect on their own learning and on their place in the Kingdom of God, then the time spent on this is an important part of learning. You will notice that much of the class time we are suggesting will come from English, social studies, and Bible classes, but we will be happy to rethink any of this.

Andrea: How do we know this will work? Do we have any way of assessing the value of this project?

Dave: The committee talked about assessment, and this is what we came up with. Since we will begin only with our incoming ninth graders, it will take four years until we have gone through one complete phase. We should survey the students at the end of their senior year to determine whether they believe it was worthwhile. We also should survey students five years after graduation and ask the same questions. So, the truth is that we won't know for some time whether what we plan is really worth doing. Isn't that true of much of what we do in teaching?

Joy: Might the parents object to our giving the Myers-Briggs Assessment to our ninth graders? Is it being done anywhere else?

Dave: Manchester High School in Connecticut has been using it with eleventh graders since 2001. They report that after the results have been generated the counselor has a ninety minute discussion with the class explaining how the results might affect the students' interests, choice of colleges, and future career. San Diego School District, serving more than 135,000 students, gives the test to ninth graders and to new faculty. Those who use the test provide positive reports, but we haven't heard from those who have had negative experiences.

Tom: We might want to provide an opportunity for parents to take the Myers-Briggs themselves. They would have to be willing to pay the cost, but it would alleviate any concerns they have and might even help some of them. The same is true of teachers who have never taken that test.

Life after High School

Bonnie: *We've been focusing our discussion on the Myers-Briggs. What about the other part of the plan?*

Joe: *Aside from the time it all takes, I think the plan includes a lot of good ideas. I think I would have been helped if my high school had done that, and it seems clear to me that Dave also agrees.*

Tom: *This has been a worthwhile discussion. It isn't the end, by any means; but the committee has started us off on a good note with this plan. We would like to have this, or something similar, in place for our grade nine students by October. Thanks, everyone.*

When preparing students for life after high school we have to think about what they will do and also how they will do it. This means that students need models and mentors, and they also need clear advice about the next steps.

It may be a surprise to learn how little parents, even those who are college educated, actually know about higher education opportunities for their children. They often look to high school guidance counselors to provide the advice their children need, but these counselors at times have their own biases. Recently a guidance counselor at a Christian high school said to a young woman we know who is an outstanding student, "You say that you are looking for a college that has a good pre-law program because you want to be an attorney. Perhaps it would be better to find a program that will help you become a para-legal. That way you can combine what you do with being a wife and mother."

Last year a group of high school students asked us to sit with them to discuss higher education options. They wanted to remain in the northwestern part of the U.S., and their parents were advising them to look at state universities since they would likely not qualify for financial aid. After a discussion concerning financial aid, we asked the students, "What are you really looking at when you try to select a college?" Several answered that they use the *Rate My Professor* website. They said that they select their major interest area and then determine how many of the professors have high scores in interesting classes, high scores in helpfulness and low scores in easiness. The students said they wanted to get a good education.

We were impressed with the desire of these students to be challenged. But, we were concerned about the limited information they had about choosing the next step. Most colleges and universities send staff members to high schools or to college fairs to draw students. We suggest that high schools ask for faculty representatives to make presentations to their classes.

This is an unusual step, but it can impact the way students understand the difference between a university where faculty see themselves as researchers and one where faculty see their role as continued development of students.

Is college for me?

When President Barack Obama said that college was important for people to enter the middle class, he was criticized by some for being elitist. It is true that some people should take paths other than college in their lives, but it is also true that college can be an excellent way to discover how we can best use the gifts God has given us.

We believe that every student should at least consider furthering education beyond high school, partly because it is such a good economic investment and partly because it opens doors for students to consider what God is calling them to do.

Over the past several years, there has been a great deal of discussion about the high cost of university education. It is absolutely true that college is expensive, but study after study demonstrates that the money spent on a university education is well worth it. A four year degree is more valuable today than ever before. The United States Labor Department provided statistics to the Economic Policy Institute in Washington D.C., and the results demonstrated that in 2012 Americans with a four year degree made ninety-eight percent more per hour than those without a degree. Analysts point out that this is higher than ever before. For example, the wage gap was only sixty-four percent in the early 1980s.

David Autor did further analysis and claims that over the course of a life, even though college is expensive, not going to college will cost $500,000 in lost wages. Even though college students have debt, they will likely more than recoup their expenditures.

Which university should I go to? Should I start at community college to save money and get rid of my "gen eds?"

Just as we must decide whether Christian worldview is important for elementary and secondary education, we also must ask whether Christian education is important at the university level. The debates have striking parallels. Those who attend secular schools emphasize that they have an opportunity to share faith that Christian schools do not allow. Those that attend faith-based institutions emphasize that Christian worldview continues to be developed in a way that becomes more fully owned by students. There are merits to both arguments.

As college professors, we emphasize that most students do not really benefit from the prestige of an institution or even from the wide variety of majors that huge schools offer. Our observation is that students do best in an environment where they are known and where they will, in turn, know those that teach them. This can occur in a wide variety of institutions, but it is something that high school students and their advisors should keep in mind as they make choices. Over and over, we have seen students attend excellent schools but just get lost in the numbers. If a large institution has been attentive to this challenge and can explain how they work to minimize the impact of their size on the average eighteen-year-old, then that institution could be a very good spot for continued development of a student.

Another thing we see is high school students concerned about finances making the choice to start at a community college to "get my 'gen eds' out of the way." While we understand financial concerns there are two things that give us pause about this approach.

First, it is in the very first year of university life that so many relationships are built, and institutions today put a great deal of work into helping students make the adjustments necessary to university life. If a student transfers as a junior, that student will often lose much of that individual attention.

Second, "getting gen eds out of the way" is a sad way to look at education. All universities require math, humanities, art, social science, and so forth but there are many different ways to fulfill these requirements. "Getting them out of the way" is the least effective approach a student can take. For humanities a student can take a history course that the student does not want to take, or that same student could take a humanities philosophy class that opens a whole new way of thinking (or vice versa). Selecting these courses carefully with individual attention from an advisor is a much better way of moving through university life.

A different cost-conscious approach would be for a student coming out of high school to consider taking a "gap year." This would give the student time to earn some money and also time to think more carefully about what he or she really wants from university life. This isn't the best choice for everyone, but in the students we have seen this is a better choice than "getting gen eds out of the way." Even if finances are not the key for a student, a gap year can still be very beneficial. High school graduates grow tremendously from programs like *Mission Year* or *AmeriCorps*. These programs give young people time to think, and they increase focus for a number of high school graduates.

Once I get there, what should I major in?

Parents are often concerned about their child's major, but as faculty we think there is way too much emphasis put on this choice. For most people, in most but not all fields, a university major did not translate directly into a particular job. Liberal arts majors help students learn to write, to think, and to assess evidence. In addition, though, there is something else that too few students make use of that can impact future earnings: internships. Internships help students apply what they are learning in the classroom to the field of work. Furthermore, they help students build networks and learn about possible jobs. Probably most importantly, they help students understand fairly quickly what sorts of jobs they might *not* want to do. Attending a university that emphasizes internships in a liberal arts environment can be a very practical approach for many high school graduates.

Our own bias is that students should select colleges where their worldview, whatever that may be, will be challenged and developed. This is all the more important when our students are starting to think about how their work will be part of what God is calling them to in the world.

Tom: We've been talking about university choices and the issue of work. Matthew Kaemingk is the director of the Fuller Institute for Theology and Northwest Culture. He has spent time thinking about faith and work, and today he is talking with us via Skype as we work on our plan for the students. Matt, we have heard the phrase "theology of work." What does that mean?

Matt: It helps to break it down. Theology can be defined quite simply as exploring the nature, desires, and activity of God. Theological questions include: Who is God? What does God want? What is God doing? On the other hand, work can be broadly defined as the creative actions human beings take in order to achieve a desired outcome which most often includes a wage of some sort.

Therefore to engage in a "theology of work" is to put those two things together. It is, in essence, to understand our work through the lens of God's nature, desires, and activity. To engage in a theology of work one might ask the following question, "If God desires justice, beauty, flourishing, or healing, how might that desire impact the way I approach my daily work?"

The assumption here is that God matters not only on Sunday but on Monday as well. On Sunday, we learn and sing about God's nature, God's desires, and God's actions. On Monday, we do our best to reflect, honor, and enact in our work God's nature, desires, and actions.

Bonnie: Parents often want their children to be successful which often means focusing on high test scores, getting into excellent universities, and getting jobs that are influential as lawyers, doctors, or business people. What do you think about this?

Matt: I have three things to say about this. First, we are stewards of our children, not owners. These children belong to God and God's church, not to us. This is obviously a very counter-cultural belief, one that might grate on our biological ties to our kids. While it might be received as bad news, it is actually very comforting to know that parents are not ultimately responsible for their child's spiritual, intellectual, or financial success. God is sovereign over their lives; we are their stewards, and caretakers. It is a serious vocation to be parent, but it is one that is given by a higher parent who knows our children's true name.

Second, one of the best gifts we can give our children is the ability to critically deconstruct the world's perverted understanding of success. This is not an endorsement of laziness or a lack of excellence but a questioning of what the true goal or the "true north" of our lives really is. Historically education in the West has always been focused on the cultivation of wisdom and virtue. Contemporary education on the other hand is focused on the formation of a workforce that can produce and consume with efficiency and power. Education in the former age was shaped by the biblical worldview, while education in the later age was shaped by the capitalistic worldview.

Third, if they are college bound, how do we want our children to enter college? With a spirit of curiosity and wonder or with a spirit of bare competition? One spirit will only learn the immediate facts and answers that are required to get ahead. The other spirit will lead to a lifetime of learning and investigation, a life that can grow, adapt, and change as marketplace demands shift.

Dave: Are there things you would encourage us to focus on as we think about preparing the next generation for the challenges that they will face?

Matt: The next generation will change jobs and vocations multiple times throughout their lives. They will live through tremendous levels of change at *a rapid pace. In order to endure and flourish they will need rich, rooted, and creative theology, a strong and vibrant faith community, and a clear vision of what it means to be a Christian in a post-Christian world. They cannot be sheltered from the difficult challenges of work, life, and faith. They must be introduced to the hard questions earlier. They must learn to wrestle. They need adults who don't have all of the answers but are willing to wrestle with the big questions as well— folks who can model wrestling with faith and doubt, courage and fear, in a way that is faithful and gracious.*

Finally, there are some very practical things that high school students should keep in mind if they are thinking about college life. One wonderful gift for college bound students is *1001 Things Every College Student Needs to Know: (Like Buying Your books Before Exams Start)* by Harry Harrison. Harrison emphasizes the practical and the mundane, but he does so with humor, wisdom, and grace. If more of our students had followed his advice they would have seen even more academic success earlier on.

In addition, a group of Christian university graduates offer these pieces of wisdom.

- What you do for a job is not who you are.
- Life is long, and there is always time to pursue something new.
- Figure out what matters most to you. Everything else is peripheral.
- If you are depressed, get help. You are not weak, and others can help you make life's challenges manageable.
- Being vulnerable is not a weakness.
- Credit cards are evil.
- Doing well in class means being able to adapt to how different teachers teach so get to know your professors.
- Mistakes are not the end of the world.
- College flies by, so do all the stupid little things you think you're too cool to do.
- Take more math. Take more math!
- Time spent on study abroad and internships is worth it. You will never have so much free time again.

Life after High School

- Enjoy staying up late, being quirky, and having commitments that last only fifteen weeks.
- Try to figure out what adds value to your life, but do not obsess over it.
- No one has all the answers. The only satisfying response to life's questions is the one you find yourself.
- Even though college courses are tougher than high school, they can be more fun. You might even get better grades than you did in high school.
- Ask questions about your schedule/academic plan. There are often multiple ways to satisfy a requirement, and you might prefer the alternative over the mainstream option. For example, your "fine arts" requirement might be satisfied by a class like technical theatre. You don't have to take an introduction to fine arts unless you want to.
- Some of those skills that professors harp about like writing well and writing succinctly can really help you succeed in the workplace and set you apart from your peers.
- Take some time to go to evening lectures or participate in extracurricular events in your classes or departments. They're great ways to connect with classmates, professors, and hear about some interesting topics not always covered in the courses offered by the school.
- The most important thing you'll learn in college is not what to think, but rather how to think critically and find solutions to problems.

Further resources

Mission Year http://missionyear.org/

AmeriCorps http://www.nationalservice.gov/programs/americorps

Languages and Faith by Bendi Benson Schrambach, PhD, (University of California), Professor of Modern Languages and Culture

Why should Christians study other cultures or learn another language? Our God is a God of diversity. Having formed mountains and seashores, tulips and daisies, caterpillars and camels, He fashioned His crowned jewel: humanity – red and yellow, black and white. There is no cultural "them" and "us" to God: He "loves the little children [and adults] of the world." We should likewise. Yet gleaning an understanding of a different culture is nearly impossible without some knowledge of its language. The very tool through which humans process thought, language both reflects and informs its culture's vision of the world.

The Bible attests to the power of words: the Lord *spoke* the world into existence; Jesus is the *Word* who became flesh; Abram is renamed Abraham and Simon, Peter, foretelling the pillars of faith they would be. Believers are exhorted to praise the Lord and admonished to never take his name in vain. Even the arrival of the Holy Spirit underscores this biblical priority. One easy way to integrate faith into language study is via the Word of God. Students are often familiar with Bible passages in English. Seeing them in another language not only teaches them the unique lexicon of Christianity, but also grants them a new perspective on God's Word. It is surprising how differently a passage can appear in another language. This activity allows students to consider the biblical lesson with new eyes.

The benefits of learning another language are myriad. First and foremost, language learning helps us to become attentive to the words that we use – in any language – and choose our words with care. It allows us to consider things from a different perspective and grants us insight into the values and priorities of our own culture. Language learning also fosters humility; deprived of the ability to charm or impress via rhetorical prowess, language apprentices are reminded of their human fallibility. Finally, language acquisition, accomplished through repeated experiences of trial and error, builds perseverance.

Language skills and corresponding cultural sensitivity are ultimately tools, the aim of which is communication and understanding. Such understanding, as Christians, should enable us to better "love [our] neighbor as [our]self" (Leviticus 19:18).

12

Life-long Learning

"Why did you leave your legal practice to become a teacher?" asked Sue.

Joy smiled and said, "I get that a lot and it is difficult to explain without sounding a bit strange. I knew I was successful enough in the corporate law firm where I practiced; but day after day, I saw my life as mostly concerned about other peoples' money.

"I began to realize that even though I had a great salary and the respect of my colleagues, I really didn't like my life. It took me a couple of years to make the decision to go into teaching. Along the way I did a lot of study about faith, law, and political life while asking whether Christians should ever compromise in the field of politics."

"Are you glad you made this choice?" asked Sue.

"On most days I really am," answered Joy. "Although there are days when I think that what we are trying to do here is just too difficult. Most of the time I believe our efforts are worthwhile and that we are engaged in something important, and I am amazed at all I have learned since I came here. I guess we never are too old to learn."

"Well, that's good. Because I've heard that great teachers are great learners." Sue replied.

As college professors with decades of experience watching our students graduate and move into adult life we've noticed something that is both interesting and sad. Some students can get straight A's in high school, move through college graduating with honors, get a good job, and then never pick up a book again. They will make arguments without evidence and turn into people who are easily swayed by culture. On the other hand, we've seen people that did not go to college who read vociferously and continue to push themselves in various ways over the course of their lives. They challenge themselves and others, and they seek to learn about God's world in a variety of ways.

The difference between these types of people is not college; it is the propensity for life-long learning. The question is, how do we encourage this kind of learning in students? It can be hard, because sometimes life-long learning is threatening.

Life-long learning often means changing our minds. For Christians, the words *uncertainty* and *compromise* can be very scary. If we believe the Bible is the inspired and unerring Word of God, and if we are strong in our faith, how can we have uncertainty? Even worse, once we become certain of something about a Christian life, how scary to change our minds or to engage in compromise!

Joy continued, "You know, it's funny you say that about learning. This summer I was on an airplane listening in on the conversation between two women in my row. They were both teachers and both Christians, but it wasn't clear to me what sort of school they taught in. One of them was talking about a book she was reading that explained human beings had a gene for a tail but that gene had been switched off. She said to her friend, 'Did you know that? What does that mean about God? Is evolution real? It blew my mind!' Her friend said, 'Don't even tell me about that. I know what I know and people do not have a gene for tails!' It was all I could to keep from interrupting them and talking about what it means to trust God in the learning that we do all our lives. Instead I pretended to sleep."

One of the greatest gifts God has given to humankind is the gift of curiosity. God has made us to be very curious because the more we wonder about ourselves, about our thinking, and about this great creation around us, the more we will want to study and learn. We come to know God in part by learning about ourselves and about the world God gave us for our home. The more we know about ourselves and our world the greater our desire will be to care for our own bodies and for our world, which is something God has commanded us to do.

We make a mistake if we ever imply to our students that learning begins and ends in school. All of life is learning, at every age, whether or not we are in school. If we teachers are to be all that God created us to be, then surely we will want to continue learning throughout our lives.

Life-long Learning

For many of us, life-long learning happens by spurts rather than in a nice, smooth line. Even learning more about our own faith happens in different seasons of faith, not once but over and over again. Jesus talked about finding life, losing life, and then finding life again. Much of learning is like that with our gathering information about a topic, wondering about it, setting it aside, and later finally being able to say, "Oh, I didn't understand that before, but now I get it."

Learning to think is not the greatest difficulty in becoming life-long learners. Our greatest difficulty comes, rather, from giving up our old ways of thinking. Throughout childhood and into adulthood we are constantly trying to make sense of the world. Unfortunately, making sense is not the same thing as being correct. In *Changing Minds: The Art and Science of Changing Our Own and Other People's*, Gardner describes the kinds of, often false, theories that children and young people develop on their own.

- Intuitive theories of matter: Heavier objects fall to the ground more rapidly than lighter objects.

- Intuitive theories of life: If it is moving, it is alive. If it is still, it is dead. If it eats, it is an animal.

- Intuitive theories of mind: All organisms have minds. The more that they resemble us in outward appearance, the more their minds are like ours. When you talk to a monkey or dog, that animal is far more likely to understand you than a fish or snake would be able to.

- Intuitive theories of human relations: Individuals who are big are powerful. It is desirable to be on their side. If you can't seize power yourself, align yourself with those who wield power.[43]

We learn to correct some of our own theories very easily. Young children are convinced that tall people or fat people are older than short or thin people and easily learn to correct that theory themselves. Other theories children make for themselves have certain plausibility, and it is very difficult to help them understand the truth. Remember when you thought that lightning caused thunder? Lightning is often followed by thunder and certainly seems, on logical grounds, to cause it. Even though you now understand the relationship between lightning and thunder, you still might flinch when you hear thunder's loud crack.

---

43. Gardner, *Changing Minds: The Art and Science of Changing Our Own and Other People's*, 55.

As adults, the theories we make for ourselves are extremely difficult to change because they are usually closely tied to our emotions. They are even more difficult to change if we have made a public commitment to them. People with more authoritarian personalities or with a more absolutist approach to life are even more likely to cling to the theories they have made for themselves. If we are to continue learning throughout our lives, we must be willing to correct our theories.

What are the characteristics of people who continue learning throughout their lives?

There has been a great deal written about adults who continue to learn well on into their later years. Some people believe that being interested in learning throughout life is a characteristic with which one is born. Others say a zest for life-long learning develops because of events that happen in one's family, community, or school experiences and therefore can to some extent be learned. Both are correct. It surely is easier to become a life-long learner if one is born with a particular proclivity for doing so. It also is easier to become a life-long learner if one is raised in an environment in which people express their own curiosity about things.

When they studied 1,500 learners for the purpose of discovering characteristics of effective life-long learners, Ruth Deakin-Crick and others identified the following:

1. Effective learners know that through practice their minds can get stronger just as their bodies. They gain pleasure and self-esteem from knowing things.

2. Effective learners love to see connections between what they are learning and what they already know.

3. Effective learners love to challenge what they are being told and ask questions because they are curious.

4. Effective learners admit when they don't know something and like a challenge. They know that learning is sometimes difficult and can readily recover from the frustration of making mistakes.

5. Effective learners like playing with ideas and using their imagination.

6. Effective learners like to share their difficulties in learning with others so that they can learn from them.

7. Effective learners know that there are other people around them in the wider community who can help them learn.

Deakin-Crick and her colleagues found the following in less effective learners:

1. Less effective learners tend to think that people are either smart or stupid and there isn't much one can do about it. They don't like to admit their confusion or mistakes. They don't value challenging situations as opportunities to learn more.
2. Less effective learners depend on other people for their sense of self as a learner. They prefer specific rules or assignments that tell them exactly what to do.
3. Less effective learners give up easily.
4. Less effective learners often do not have strong learning homes, families, and communities to support their learning.

We must not confuse becoming an effective life-long learner or thinker with becoming an avid reader. Among the many famous people who have had serious difficulty with reading are: Winston Churchill, Leonardo da Vinci, Albert Einstein, Anthony Hopkins, John Irving, and Agatha Christie. There are people who speak of the "gift of dyslexia" because it allowed and forced them to think in new and creative ways.

Certainly these people can be characterized as life-long learners in spite of their reading or spelling difficulties. Even young adolescents who read well may find learning from other sources easier than learning from reading. We live in such a fast-paced world and are constantly bombarded with newly discovered information. In such a world, children need to come to understand the important place learning must have throughout their lives. The ability to learn how to learn is one of the most important ways we have of coping with this world. Children who develop skills for life-long learning will carry with them the resilience, creativity, critical curiosity, learning awareness, and interdependence they will need in order to continue to grow in knowledge about this world God has given us.

Teaching to Justice, Citizenship, and Civic Virtue

How can teachers encourage their students to become effective life-long learners?

It is possible to develop a tendency for life-long learning. A tendency is something that one does without thinking. A tendency begins with a commitment that arises from a worldview. The tendency is a response to that commitment, practiced over and over, until it becomes part of one's self. It is a commitment to a particular action that is practiced so often it becomes as natural as breathing.

There are especially wise teachers who understand that the way they ask questions on a test can lead students into life-long learning. Here is an example developed by Stephen Janssen, teacher at Knox Christian School, Bowmanville, Ontario:

- Think of yourself as one of the following: A parent twenty-five years from now with school-age children wanting to watch T.V., go to movies, and listen to music deciding what your little ones should or shouldn't be exposed to; or a college student living on your own having to decide on what TV, which movies, and which music is appropriate for you as a disciple of Christ.

- Develop a statement and/or method by which you can ensure that all involved can live in obedience, and participate in the world without being worldly. What will be called appropriate, and what is inappropriate?

Among the many suggestions Ruth Deakin-Crick makes to help students increase their awareness of themselves as changing and learning and to increase their creativity as a learner are the following:

- Think of yourself as a lifelong learner!
- Think about how your body gets stronger and more fit with exercise and start an exercise regime for your mind and brain.
- Try guessing at solutions before working them out; see how good your guess was.
- Make up characters and situations in which the concepts, ideas and facts in your learning come to life for you: write or imagine scripts and scenes.

- Make mind maps with labels or draw "trees" with "meaning branches" to show how possibilities multiply when you think about alternative scenarios.

Keep It Small, Keep It Real: Helping Students Write About Faith by Nichole Sheets, PhD, (University of Utah), Creative writing professor, Pushcart Prize nominee 2011

I grew up in a small Baptist church full of people who love to testify. Men and women stand up and talk about how Christ came into their lives, or how God's loving presence has been revealed to them afresh. The testimony is one of the first forms of storytelling that I internalized. (Another is the parable, which is, of course, best demonstrated by paper figures on a flannelgraph board.) Stories like these, with their familiar shapes, influenced me as a young writer.

In college, I joined a nondenominational Christian group that encouraged us to hone our testimony into a three-minute presentation. The point was to have a sleek vehicle for evangelism, but the format felt limiting: my life before Christ, encountering Christ, my life after Christ. I knew that there was so much more to say.

As a writer and teacher, I'm drawn to the personal essay as a space for reflecting on and making sense out of my Christian faith. This kind of spiritual writing is more autobiographical, less devotional or didactic. I haven't outgrown the testimony. But I have found that life's complexities sometimes require other genres. The same is true for many of my students, who often have a lot to say about their relationship with God. I'd like to look at some of the challenges and benefits of spiritual writing, and some ideas for making this work in the classroom.

Challenges and benefits

Writers and teachers of writing face a familiar dilemma: words often show their flimsiness in our moments of most intense feeling. How do we put language around something as personal and intangible as faith? As an added danger, spiritual writing can be especially susceptible to cliché or a reliance on pre-packaged narratives. In *Tell It Slant*, an excellent textbook on creative nonfiction, Brenda Miller and Suzanne Paola advise that "[y]ou must remain aware of how your brand of spirituality has been depicted in the past and find a way to circumvent your reader's expectations and resistance. How do you even begin to discuss spirituality without immediately using language that has lost its meaning from overuse?"[44]

Some writers, particularly in a Christian context, may feel pressure to be positive or wrap up their story, no matter how sordid or unfinished, with a tidy bow. Maybe there's the expectation of a moral, or at least an affirmation of some kind of pithy truth: God doesn't close a door without opening a window. God doesn't give you more than you can handle. Let go, and let God. Etc. While I recognize that these sayings are often well intentioned, the bumper sticker theology doesn't usually translate into an engaging personal essay. (In my experience, it triggers eye rolls so loud you can hear them from across the classroom.)

Perhaps there's a fear that students will stray from faith if they're turned loose to explore it in writing. But honest inquiry means we risk changing our minds about what we believe. For me, and for many of my students, writing about faith is a way to live it more deeply. According to John Gage, in *The Shape of Reason*, higher-order thinking often demands that we hold contradictory ideas in our heads. Gage means that paradoxes are unavoidable when we're wrestling with difficult and important questions. One of the features I love about the essay form is that it's flexible and spacious. It's a good place for trying out ideas. When I'm engaged in this kind of spiritual writing I can have a deep and abiding Christianity even while thinking critically about the Church and its practices.

By the time students reach a writing workshop at a Christian liberal arts college, they usually have something to say either about the religion they grew up with or the lack thereof. My goal is to provide a safe space for this to happen, to reassure students that they're not being graded on their orthodoxy but on the effort they've invested and the creative risks they've taken in their work.

While students take on this challenge as writers, they're often already quite sophisticated as readers. Students can spot flat, glib, cheesy, heavy-handed, agenda-driven writing from a mile away. If nothing else, spiritual writing validates a B.S. detector as one of a writer's greatest tools.

---

44. Miller and Paola, *Tell It Slant*, 42.

Our spirituality is as squirrelly, intense, mundane, and detail-rich as the rest of our lives. Writing about our faith can deepen our curiosity and renew our sense of wonder. In Genesis 1, God creates. Writing reminds us that making something from a blank page feels like nothing short of a miracle.

What's helped

Keep it small.

In *Bird by Bird*, Anne Lamott describes the "one-inch picture frame" through which she views her work for the day. The idea is to make an unmanageable task feel more manageable. A student who sets out to write her entire spiritual autobiography may collapse under the crushing weight of her project. A student who writes about that Wednesday afternoon at church camp when she made friendship bracelets in the craft room during a thunderstorm has a more reachable goal.

Keep it real.

If there's not a moral to a student's story, if there's not a clear lesson to be learned, honor that. Better a dose of honest (and well written) uncertainty than a forced conclusion. W.H. Auden's definition of poetry as "clear writing about mixed feelings" applies to nonfiction, too.

Love the details.

Our spiritual lives aren't just dramatic moments of conversion or baptism. Much of the joy of spiritual writing, as in all writing, lies in illuminating a detail that we might have overlooked. In *A Poetry Handbook*, Mary Oliver claims that details create "texture" in our writing. "Such texture," Oliver explains, "is vital to all poetry. It is what makes the poem an experience, something much more than mere statement."[45] The same is true for creative nonfiction, a close cousin of poetry.

45. Oliver, *A Poetry Handbook*, 27.

Love your details.

One of my favorite exercises to do in any writing class is called "Things That Happen to You," from *What If? Writing Exercises for Fiction Writers*, edited by Anne Painter and Pamela Bernays. Over the course of a week or so, students make a list of ten specific things that make them angry, and ten that make them happy. An example: "The tiny acolyte, maybe six years old, wore sneakers that blinked red as he hoisted the silver Bible up on the altar." The students need not explain why they categorized these items on the "angry" or "happy." The point is to help students take an inventory of the writing material in their lives, to tune into their senses, and to heighten their powers of observation. This emphasis on specificity echoes Miller and Paola's charge in *Tell It Slant* "to find a language and a form so personal that *only you* can give us this rendition of the spiritual life."[46] What does this student notice that others might not? How does the student experience the sacred in the everyday? No detail is too small. Rather than settling for general observations like "the people on the bus," students zoom in on the purple sequined headband worn by an elderly woman leaning on her walker.

The hope is that this exercise leads students to produce a pile of images. In other words, when we write about our Christian faith, we're writing into a world full of already existing ideas, associations, terms, and images. It's easy to slip into jargon. If I write about having "quiet times" or an "accountability partner," that might make some sense to a reader familiar with certain strains of evangelical Christianity but it would be really opaque to readers of other backgrounds. I'd want to show what I mean by those terms, likely with a mix of scene and exposition, or showing and telling. Another example is when my students write about growing up "in a Christian home." I'd argue that it's one of those "overused" phrases that Miller and Paola warn us about. The shorthand of "a Christian home" doesn't tell me what I really need to know. Tell me more about this home, I say to my students. There are perhaps as many kinds of Christian homes as there are Christian families. Were you allowed to watch TV? Did you read the Bible as a family? Did you attend church together? What kind of church? What was it

---

46. Miller and Paola, *Tell It Slant*, 42.

like? Students realize a common phrase like "a Christian home" is really just the front door into a house full of memories and experiences.

Treasure the image.

An image is open-ended, a reminder that nothing means just one thing. Think of the green light at the end of Daisy Buchanan's pier in *The Great Gatsby*. What does it mean? Greed? Money? Jealousy? Nausea at the excesses of capitalism? Who knows? The image suggests so much more than it can say outright. The image keeps us rooted, lest we drift off into abstraction or fluffy platitudes.

One way to help students with their image-making is to ask them to think of an abstraction (a noun like love, hope, despair, freedom) and then write a poem or short piece of prose about that abstraction using only concrete details that appeal to the senses. Take, for example, William Wright's poem "Faith" in *Rock & Sling* 8.1. It begins:

> I have seen the face
> of God in the culled body
> of a fox picked clean in a winter field.
> . . .
> I believe in souls, for I have watched
> the high nests of wasps in the wind-stung
> elms of early fall thrive through winter[47]

Redefine.

In her book *Amazing Grace: A Vocabulary of Faith*, Kathleen Norris seeks to do what she calls *rebuilding her religious vocabulary*. Most of the chapters are short essays on words related to faith, words like: worship, seeking, judgment, neighbor. I ask my university students to pick a word related to their faith tradition and to write about their understanding of this word. Is there a memory or a story associated with it? Has their relationship to the word changed over time?

---

47. William Wright's poem *Faith* was first published in the journal *Rock and Sling*, 8:1 (2013). It appears here with permission from the author and *Rock and Sling*.

Melanie Rae Thon, one of my teachers, gave us an exercise called "The wonder of wonder." She said, "Choose a word, an idea, a condition of the senses and/or the spirit that thrills and mystifies you. Let yourself ponder all the subtle meanings of the word—its connotations and denotations, its popular and private definitions. Think about your personal experiences and associations with the word. Meditate on the images and memories that rise with the word and give yourself hours (and days) to live inside them . . . Consider words that are similar in meaning and articulate the differences between them. Does your word have a 'dark side'? Does the darkness slowly open you to even more profound insight and illumination?"

Consider the power of stories.

Literary theorist Walter Benjamin, in his beautiful essay "The Storyteller," reminds us that information has a very short shelf life, but that there's something inexhaustible about stories. Why are there four Gospels in the canonical Bible? Why not just one? Why do we reenact the Christmas pageant every year? Why do we enjoy retellings of stories we know so well?

Don't feel pressured to tell a story.

When a tree falls in a riverbed, most of it breaks down, but a few knots resist. Writer David James Duncan refers to these stubborn "cross-grained, pitch-hardened masses" as "river teeth." He forges a handy metaphor for writing: "there are hard, cross-grained whorls of human experience that remain inexplicably lodged in us, long after the straight-grained narrative material that housed them has washed away. Most of these whorls are not stories, exactly: more often they're self-contained images of shock or of inordinate empathy; moments of violence, uncaught dishonesty, tomfoolery; of mystical terror; lust; joy."[48]

Encourage students to think about their "river teeth" (for examples, consult Duncan's book *River Teeth*, and a creative nonfiction literary magazine of the same name). Sometimes we can be even more

---

48. Duncan, *River Teeth* http://www.riverteethjournal.com/about-us/river-teeth-an-introduction

free, more honest in fragments. The fragment is another antidote to pat or easy answers.

Read up.

Strong writers are strong readers. Get more ideas and inspiration from literary magazines committed to excellent writing about faith, magazines like *Image*, *Ruminate*, and *Rock & Sling* (I'm the web editor for *Rock & Sling*'s blog. So I know whereof I speak). The annual *Best American Spiritual Writing* anthology is another great place to look.

Discussion Questions

1. How do you engage in life-long learning? Do you talk to students about it?
2. In what ways do students at your school write about their faith?
3. What elements of Deakin-Crick's advice does your school already integrate? Are there others that interest you?

Conclusion

Learning from Others—Revelation and Response

Tom: This year we've spent a lot of time talking about our teaching. For the final devotion of the year, Andrea will lead us in a reflection on God's revelation and our response.

Andrea: Thank you, Tom. When I was a student in a Christian school long ago we had a Bible series called Revelation/Response. Truthfully I can't remember much about the series, but I do remember the name. The name struck with me as a way to think about how God challenges us. Here are the Scripture texts I'll be using—two from both the Old and New Testaments:

> Exodus 20: 1–3, "And God spoke all these words: [2] 'I am the Lord your God, who brought you out of Egypt, out of the land of slavery.[3] You shall have no other gods before me.'"

> Micah 6:8, "He has shown you, O mortal, what is good.
> And what does the Lord require of you?
> To act justly and to love mercy
> and to walk humbly with your God."

> Romans 8:38–39, "For I am convinced that neither death nor life, neither angels nor demons, neither the present nor the future, nor any powers, [39] neither height nor depth, nor anything else in all creation, will be able to separate us from the love of God that is in Christ Jesus our Lord."

Matthew 25: 31–46, "When the Son of Man comes in his glory, and all the angels with him, he will sit on his glorious throne. [32] All the nations will be gathered before him, and he will separate the people one from another as a shepherd separates the sheep from the goats. [33] He will put the sheep on his right and the goats on his left. [34] Then the King will say to those on his right, 'Come, you who are blessed by my Father; take your inheritance, the kingdom prepared for you since the creation of the world. [35] For I was hungry and you gave me something to eat, I was thirsty and you gave me something to drink, I was a stranger and you invited me in, [36] I needed clothes and you clothed me, I was sick and you looked after me, I was in prison and you came to visit me.' [37] Then the righteous will answer him, 'Lord, when did we see you hungry and feed you, or thirsty and give you something to drink? [38] When did we see you a stranger and invite you in, or needing clothes and clothe you? [39] When did we see you sick or in prison and go to visit you?' [40] The King will reply, 'Truly I tell you, whatever you did for one of the least of these brothers and sisters of mine, you did for me.' [41] Then he will say to those on his left, 'Depart from me, you who are cursed, into the eternal fire prepared for the devil and his angels. [42] For I was hungry and you gave me nothing to eat, I was thirsty and you gave me nothing to drink, [43] I was a stranger and you did not invite me in, I needed clothes and you did not clothe me, I was sick and in prison and you did not look after me.' [44] They also will answer, 'Lord, when did we see you hungry or thirsty or a stranger or needing clothes or sick or in prison, and did not help you?' [45] He will reply, 'Truly I tell you, whatever you did not do for one of the least of these, you did not do for me.' [46] Then they will go away to eternal punishment, but the righteous to eternal life."

Revelation/Response

This year, I've been working with a number of students who have achieved great academic and professional success. Prestige will follow them, and they are excited about their futures. This is a good thing, but I've also been struggling with my own sense of ambition and with limits—my limits, the limits of our knowledge, and the limits of our ability to "do good" and to "combat injustice." With this homily, the verses that were read and the theme of "Revelation/Response," I want to share with you the theological place to which I have come. Love Wins. I know there is a popular book out by Rob Bell of that name, but I don't mean exactly what he meant. I mean God's love wins, and so our love wins. God reveals love. We respond with love. If through that love we work in our disciplines and use our hearts and our minds to respond to God, then we do not have to worry about success, achieving, our limits, our ambition, or our prestige. None of that matters. Love Wins.

Now that might seem like common sense to you, but to me it is a huge revelation. I was raised in a theological tradition, the Reformed tradition, which did not highlight love. As a Calvinist, the themes I am more comfortable with would be: good theology wins, hard work wins, or sacrifice wins. When we consider the Scripture, it is clear that God's emphasis is love: for God so loved the world; faith, hope and love and the greatest of these is love; summation of the law and the prophets to love the Lord your God with all your heart, soul, and mind and love your neighbor as yourself.

For our consideration today I chose two passages from each of the Old and New Testaments. In each section, the theme of Revelation/Response becomes clear. I want to speak to each one separately and help illuminate what these passages might mean for your work in the future regardless of what field that work might be in.

At Midland Christian High, we talk a lot about two words: worldview and vocation. These two words capture our theme today. Worldview is our understanding of God's revelation; vocation is what we then decide to do with it. Sometimes we think of vocation as a job, but vocation is really all the ways in which we live as citizens, neighbors, parents, and workers.

In the Old Testament, God speaks, "I am the Lord your God," and the prophet Micah tells us what that means for us—we will do justice, love mercy, and walk humbly with God.

Micah is such an interesting book for us to study because his concerns parallel things we see in our own communities today. He laments the abuse of power by rulers, by the rich, and by anyone in authority. As a prophet, Micah emphasizes how wrong it is for one group to benefit at the expense of another. All of us, in all of the different ways we will work in the world, will see this. Accountants, government officials, teachers, medical personnel, office assistants, clerks in a grocery store—all of us will see abuse of power; the question is, how will we respond?

In the New Testament, Paul tells us what God has revealed: nothing can separate us from God's love. Jesus reveals to us how we must respond—we are to feed the hungry, care for the weak, and heal the sick. That's what it means to love.

In business, we must have a different driving motive for how we approach customers and workers or for how and why we move our business from place to place. We will challenge ourselves to consider what kind of commitment we must have to a neighborhood or city.

In politics, we take up tough subjects: gay marriage, gun control, and immigration. If love is first, then we still might disagree but differently. Certainly we will compromise more quickly because we will be willing to say we might not know the whole story.

In science, the purpose of our discovery and work may be re-directed. If you are a physicist, use your skills to help build infrastructure for those who suffer. A biologist can research ways to heal or ways to impact grain so that more are fed.

In our art, we can reveal truth and grace, or we can use this skill to heal. There is so much we can do with God's help.

As I have reflected on my own life and as I have talked with our alum over the years, two patterns emerge. Some of us will get so busy with our own life paying back student loans, paying the mortgage, putting kids through school, and worrying about our jobs that it becomes very easy to forget to love God's world. We get so busy we do not even see the sorrow around us. Others of us see so much sorrow we get discouraged at such a level that we can't work anymore. Everything seems to be broken.

Both of these groups, or both of these stages, have different antidotes; but the antidotes are rooted in the same thing: Love wins. When we are complacent, we need the community around us to remind us that God requires our response—vocation. When we are despondent, we need our communities to remind us of God's revelation that He is the Master—worldview.

Worldview/vocation.

Revelation/response.

Love wins,

Amen.

Bibliography

Arnett, Jeffrey. *Emerging Adulthood: The Winding Road from the Late Teens Through the Twenties*. New York:Oxford University Press, 2002.

Baumeister, Roy, et al. "Does High Self-esteem Cause Better Performance, Interpersonal Success, Happiness, or Healthier Lifestyles?" *Psychological Science in the Public Interest* (2003) 4: 1–44.

Bransford, John, et al. *How People Learn*. 2nd edition. Washington DC:National Academies Press, 2002.

Bochner, Stephen. "Cross-cultural Differences in the Self Concept," *Journal of Cross-Cultural Psychology* (1994) 25.2: 273–283.

Brooks, David. *The Social Animal: The Hidden Sources of Love, Character, and Achievement*. New York: Random House, 2011.

Brummelman, Eddie, et al. "'That's Not Just Beautiful–That's Incredibly Beautiful!': The Adverse Impact of Inflated Praise on Children with Low Self-esteem." *Psychological Science* (2014) 25.3: 728–735.

"Consensus: 97% of Climate Scientists Agree." In NASA. http://climate.nasa.gov/scientific-consensus. Accessed December 12, 2013.

Deakin-Crick, Ruth. *Learning Power in Practice: A Guide for Teachers*. Thousand Oaks:Sage Publications Ltd, 2006.

Deakin-Crick, Ruth, et al. "Developing an Effective Lifelong Learning Inventory: The Effective Learning Profile (ELLI)". Center for Assessment Studies, University of Bristol. Unpublished manuscript, 2002.

Dobbs, David. "Beautiful Brains," *National Geographic* (2011) October: 36–59.

Du Bois, William Edward Burghardt. *The Souls of Black Folk*. New York: Dover Books, 1903.

Duncan, David James. *River Teeth: Stories and Writings*. New York: The Dial Press, 1996. http://www.riverteethjournal.com/about-us/river-teeth-an-introduction

Ekman, Paul. "Moods, Emotions, and Traits" In *The Nature of Emotion*, edited by P. Ekman & R. J. Davidson, 56–58. New York: Oxford University Press, 1994.

Essenburg, Michael. *Empowering Christian Leaders and Organizations to Close the Rhetoric/reality Gap Now*. http://closethegapnow.org Accessed April 12, 2014.

Gardner, Howard. *Changing Minds: The Art and Science of Changing Our Own and Other People's*. Boston:Harvard Business Review Press, 2006.

Giedd, Jay. "Frontline Interview." National Institute of Mental Health, 2011.

"Guidelines." In Center for Public Justice. www.cpjustice.org Accessed March 10, 2014.

Bibliography

Guthridge, George. *The Kids from Nowhere: The Story Behind the Arctic Educational Miracle.* Anchorage: Alaska Northwest Books, 2006.

Joldersma, Clarence and Gloria Stronks. *Educating for Shalom.* Grand Rapids:Wm. B Eerdmans, 2004.

King Jr, Martin Luther. "Beyond Vietnam," Address delivered to The Clergy and Laymen Concerned about Vietnam at Riverside Church, New York City, New York, 1967.

Lewis, Clive Staples. *The Four Loves.* New York: Harcourt, Brace & Co., 1960.

MacDonald, Geoff & Mark Leary. "Why Does Social Exclusion Hurt? The Relationship Between Social and Physical Pain." *Psychological Bulletin* (2005) 131.2: 202–223.

Miller, Brenda and Suzanne Paola. *Tell It Slant.* 2nd ed. New York: McGraw Hill, 2012.

Neff, Kristin. "Self-compassion, Self-esteem, and Well-being." *Social and Personality Psychology Compass (2011)* 5.1: 1–12.

Neff, Kristin, and Christopher Germer. "A Pilot Study and Randomized Controlled Trial of the Mindful Self-compassion Program." *Journal of Clinical Psychology* (2013)1.17: dii: 10. 1002/jclp.21923.

Neff, Kristin and Pitman McGehee. "Self-compassion and Psychological Resilience Among Adolescents and Young Adults." *Self and Identity (2010)* 9: 225–240.

Neff, Kristin and Roos Vonk. "Self-compassion Versus Global Self-esteem: Two Different Ways of Relating to Oneself." *Journal of Personality* (2009) 77.1: 23–50.

Nouwen, Henri, Donald McNeill, and Douglas Morrison. *Compassion: A Reflection on the Christian Life.* New York: Doubleday, 1982.

Nouwen, Henri. *Life of the Beloved.* New York: The Crossroad Publishing Company, 1992.

Oliver, Mary. *A Poetry Handbook.* Orlando: Harcourt, 1994.

Pennings, Ray, et al. *Cardus Education Survey.* 2011. http://www.cardus.ca/research/education/publications/surveys/

Ross, Lee. "The Intuitive Psychologist and His Shortcomings: Distortions in the Attribution Process." *Advances in Experimental Social Psychology* (1997) 10: 173–220.

Stronks, Gloria Goris and Douglas Blomberg. *A Vision with a Task: Christian Schooling for Responsive Discipleship.* Grand Rapids, MI: Baker Books, 1993.

Stronks, Julia and Gloria Goris Stronks. *Families Living in the Fabric of Faithfulness: Parents and Children Describe What Works,* 2004. http://www.whitworth.edu/academic/department/politicalscience/faculty/stronksjulia/pdf/fabricoffaithfulness.pdf

Taliaferro, Charles. "Love." In *Being Good: Christian Virtues for Everyday Life,* edited by M.W. Austin & R. Douglas Geivett. Grand Rapids, MI: Wm. B. Eerdmans Publishing Co., 2012.

Twenge, Jean. *Generation Me.* New York: Free Press, 2006.

Twenge, Jean and W. Keith Campbell. "Increases in Positive Self-views among High School Students." *Psychological Science* (2008) 19.11: 1082–1086.

Volf, Miroslav. *A Public Faith: How Followers of Christ Should Serve the Common Good.* Grand Rapids:Brazos Press, 2013.

Williams, Kip, and Steve Nida. "Ostracism: Consequences and Coping." *Psychological Science* (2011) 20.2: 71–75.

Wood, Joanne, Elaine Perunovic, and John Lee. "Positive Self-statements: Power for Some, Peril for Others." *Psychological Science* (2007) 20:7: 860–866.

Wydick, Bruce. "Cost-Effective Compassion: The 10 Most Popular Strategies for Helping the Poor," *Christianity Today* (2012) 56. 2: 24.

www.ingramcontent.com/pod-product-compliance
Lightning Source LLC
Chambersburg PA
CBHW071441160426
43195CB00013B/1989